ACTION SPANISH

FOR

Law Enforcement

Spanish for Beginners

Michael Kane
Coastal Bend College

Barbara Welder
Coastal Bend College

Dalel Cortés
The Mexican Immersion Center

Prentice
Hall

Upper Saddle River, New Jersey 07458

Library of Congress Cataloging-in-Publication Data

Kane, Michael.
  Action Spanish for law enforcement : Spanish for beginners / Michael Kane, Barbara Welder, Dalel Cortés
    p. cm. 1 videorecording + compact disk.
  Includes index.
  English and Spanish.
  ISBN 0-13-085205-8
    1. Spanish lanuage—Conversation and phrase books (for police) I. Welder, Barbara.
II. Cortés, Dalel. III. Title.

PC4120.P64 K36 2002
468.3'421'024363—dc21

2001045943

Publisher: Jeff Johnston
Executive Editor: Kim Davies
Production Editor: Lori Dalberg, Carlisle Publishers Services
Production Liaison: Barbara Marttine Cappuccio
Director of Production & Manufacturing: Bruce Johnson
Managing Editor: Mary Carnis
Manufacturing Buyer: Cathleen Petersen
Design Director: Cheryl Asherman
Cover Design Coordinator: Miguel Ortiz
Cover Designer: Joseph DaPinho
Marketing Manager: Jessica Pfaff
Assistant Editor: Sarah Holle
Editorial Assistant: Korrine Dorsey
Composition: Carlisle Communications, Ltd.
Printing and Binding: Banta Harrisonburg

Pearson Education LTD.
Pearson Education Australia PTY, Limited
Pearson Education Singapore, Pte. Ltd.
Pearson Education North Asia Ltd.
Pearson Education Canada, Ltd.
Pearson Educacíon de Mexico, S.A. de C.V.
Pearson Education—Japan
Pearson Education Malaysia, Pte. Ltd.

10 9 8 7 6 5 4 3 2 1
ISBN 0-13-085205-8

To Carolyn Kane, Amos Welder, Jorge Sernas,
and
to all Criminal Justice Professionals, past, present, and future.

CONTENTS

PREFACE

Action Spanish for Law Enforcement began in the summer of 1996. Our task was to prepare a living "action-oriented text" which would address the needs of real law enforcement-criminal justice professionals. We decided that the book must have four elements: a) **authentic law enforcement language** and situations must be used; b) **no grammar** explanations would be appropriate; c) **an action-oriented video** and audio CD must accompany the project; and d) **many cognates or words with similar looks** and meaning would be the basis for easy to master Action Scenes and Scenarios of each chapter.

The book was then piloted for two years by Spanish for Law Enforcement classes. Students had adequate time to provide input for changes. Our support law enforcement personnel also provided help to make the language authentic, (i.e., sound like real-life Spanish).

Finally, the project spanned to three authors in two countries, which has given this project a fully international dimension. Our greatest challenge was adapting this text to include practical Spanish. The focus is in using Standard versions with some non-standard (slang) notations. We would hope that instructors would understand the difficulty of writing a universal text for all situations that would include consideration for all varieties of Spanish. Because of this impossibility, we hope that instructors will feel free to substitute regional and local variations of Spanish to help students reach their goals. Naturally, familiar forms and slang should be adapted as needed.

In any class, both instructors and students must feel that the text, video, and audio CD material are geared to meet their needs. We hope that we have succeeded in reaching that goal.

Michael Kane, Division Chairperson of Protective Services, Coastal Bend College, Beeville, Texas

Barbara M. Welder, Professor of Spanish, Coastal Bend College, Beeville, Texas

Dalel Cortés, Director, Mexican Immersion Center, Cuernavaca, México.

ACKNOWLEDGMENTS

We are grateful to the following people who helped make this project possible:

Kim Davies, Executive Editor, Prentice-Hall

Steven R. Brubaker of S & JB Productions and his staff in Tulsa, Oklahoma.

Leroy Peña, Dallas Police Department, Dallas, Texas

Eugenio Palomares-González, Mexican Immersion Center, Cuernavaca México

Ron Van Slooten, Victoria Police Department, Victoria, Texas.

The authors would also like to thank the following people who reviewed this book: Manuel E. Hays, Denver Police Department, Denver, CO; Jorge E. Gaytan, Houston Police Department, Houston, TX; Johnny E. Perkins, Brevard Community College, Melbourne, FL; Pedro Crescente, Brevard Community College, Melbourne, FL; Nancy Zarenda, Rio International Language Service, Marina del Rey, CA; Frank Afflitto, University of Memphis, Memphis, TN; and Alex del Carmen, University of Texas–Arlington, Arlington, TX.

INSTRUCTOR GUIDELINES

CHAPTER OUTLINE

1. *Action Scene*. **The core of the text.** The student has the opportunity to complete the investigation in which he may memorize or read questions to compile the action data.

   Action Scene: Part I contains basic informational questions.

   Action Scene: Investigation has more complex questions the student may either memorize or read.

2. *Action Scene Cognates*. Incorporates words of same origin with similar meaning for easy mastery of the scene. By using these cognates, the student may engage in active use on the *very first day*.

3. *Action Scene Vocabulary*. Helps facilitate students to master the Action Scene.

4. *Expanded Vocabulary*. Offers a supplemental, **optional** use of words and phrases connected to the Action Scene. The instructor may use this section for additional vocabulary.

5. *Action Scene Structural Exercise*. Helps the student with immediate recall and reinforcement of the Action Scene.

6. *Action Scenarios*. Develops the student's communicative skills through guided role-playing related to the situation.

7. *Cultural Notes*. These cultural notes highlight Hispanic customs and lend some background information on traditions, beliefs and laws in the Spanish-speaking world.

8. *Action Cards*. Quick reference cards which can be used on a clipboard.

A NOTE TO THE INSTRUCTOR

The language and the cultural notes address generalizations, and they are not meant to address all people from *all Spanish-speaking countries*. Rather, it is hoped these notes will assist law enforcement personnel with some insight in daily communication. *Instructors and students should feel free to substitute from their own linguistic and cultural experiences.*

Special Attention to the Following Features:

1. This program has a *non-grammatical* emphasis. Our reviewers have repeatedly requested a "No Grammar" approach. Only three points are mentioned:

   a. This book utilizes the formal "usted" form. "Tú" variations can be substituted if needed by the instructor.

   b. The direct object pronouns such as "lo, la" may be explained as applicable.

   c. The possessive pronouns such as "su, sus" may be mentioned as applicable. We do not recommend lengthly verb or structural explanations.

   d. The Action Scene reflects the same usage as the video. For example, "Está lastimada?" (female) could be changed to "Está lastimado?" if the victim is male.

2. *Authentic work language* is used in each situation. Questions and answers may vary.

3. Some *non-standard varieties* have been included because of common usage. Regional or local variations in language may be substituted.

HOW TO USE THIS BOOK

A class could be structured in this way:

1. *Preview the Action Scene.*

   Give an overview of the entire situation.

2. *Play the Action Scene Video* for the class.

   Explain what the scene is about. Do not focus so much on the answers from the person being questioned, as answers will vary.

3. *Review the Action Scene* from the text. Choral and individual response may be used.

4. *Preview selected Action Scene Cognates* from the text.

5. *Students may repeat both Action Scene Cognates and Action Scene Vocabulary.*

6. *Repeat Action Scene from text.* Ask for volunteers to respond to questions from the scene. Break this down into "chunks" of no more than 5 to 6 responses.

7. *Replay Action Scene Video or Audio CD.* The pause or stop button can be used.

   Continue through the Action Scene Structural Exercises and Action Scene Questions. These may be assigned for oral preparation.

8. *Evaluation. Ask the students to prepare the Action Scene Scenarios.*

   The instructor may use the Oral Evaluation Form (Appendix E). Depending on the time available, students may be asked to memorize or read the Action Scenarios.

9. For variety, discuss any cultural notes or other items that would apply.

Law Enforcement: A Short Course

GREETINGS/COURTESY

Greetings	Saludos
Hello.	Hola.
Good morning. Good day.	Buenos días.
Good afternoon.	Buenas tardes.
Good evening.	Buenas noches.
How are you?	¿Como está?
Please.*	Por favor.
Good-bye.	Adiós.

---

*"Please" = "por favor" is very important when asking for anything.

AGGRESSIVE ACTS

There are some of the words and phrases that the officer will be expected to be familiar with that would alert him/her of aggressive acts being considered or about to be initiated by the individual.

IMPORTANT: The officer is using the "tú" familiar form.
The officer may also use the "usted" polite form.

Commands	Los mandatos "Tú" (familiar)
Disarm him/her.	Desármalo. (la)
Jump him.	Sáltalo. (la)
Shoot him/her.	Dispárale.
Beat him/her.	Pégale.
Take his/her gun.	Quítale la pistola. (agarra-non-standard)
Hit him.	Pégale.
Kick him.	Patéalo. (la)
Run.	Córrele. Arráncate.
Step on it. (car)	Dále gas.
Stab him.	Pícalo. Córtalo.
Stop him.	Páralo.

Weapons	Las Armas
pistol	pistola
rifle	rifle
shotgun	escopeta
switchblade, clasp knife	navaja
knife	cuchillo (filero – non-standard)
bottle	botella

INVESTIGATION: INTERROGATIVE WORDS

The student will be able to recite common Spanish words or phrases which would assist an officer in the investigation and *identification of suspects and witnesses:*

Interrogative Words	Las palabras interrotivas
What?	¿Qué?
How?	¿Cómo?
Why?	¿Por qué?
When?	¿Cuándo?
Where?	¿Dónde?
How many?	¿Cuánta? (fem)
How much?	¿Cuánto? (masc) ¿Cuántos? (pl)
Which?	¿Cuál? ¿Cuáles? (pl)
Who?	¿Quién? ¿Quiénes? (pl)
Whose?	¿De quién? ¿De quiénes? (pl)

Family	La familia Nouns ending in "o" are masc. - "a" are fem.
aunt, uncle	tío (a).
boyfriend/girlfriend	novio (a).
brother/sister	hermano, (a) carnal (non-standard)
brother/sister-in-law	cuñado (a)
children	hijos
son/daughter	hijo / hija
mother	madre
father/parents	padre/padres
fiancé	prometido (a)
cousin	primo (a)
grandson/daughter	nieto (a)

husband	esposo, marido
wife	esposa
nephew/niece	sobrino (a)
father/mother-in-law	suegro (a)
relatives	parientes, familiares
grandfather/grandmother	abuelo (a)
stepfather	padrastro
stepmother	madrastra
closest friend	compadre (m) comadre (f)
close family friend	primo (m) prima (f)

Colors / Los colores

black	negro
blue	azul
beige	beige
blonde	rubio, güero (non-standard)
brown	café
brunette	moreno
gold	dorado
grey	gris
green	verde
orange	anaranjado
pink	rosado
red	rojo, colorado
silver	plata
silver plated	plateado
yellow	amarillo
white	blanco
light (referring to color)	claro
dark (referring to color)	oscuro

Clothes / La ropa

blouse	blusa
jacket	chaqueta
coat (sports coat)	saco
overcoat	abrigo
hat	sombrero
cap	gorra (la cachucha, non-standard)

shirt	camisa
pants	pantalones (el pantalón)
socks	calcetines
shoes	zapatos
gloves	guantes

FIELD INTERVIEW, TRAFFIC STOPS, ACCIDENTS

The student will be able to recite common Spanish phrases that will assist the officer conducting:

- Field Interview
- Traffic/Pedestrian Stops and
- Accident investigations

Field Interviews

Who called the police?

Do you need help?

Who is the victim?

Calm down.

What happened?

La entrevista

¿Quién llamó a la policía?

¿Necesita ayuda?

¿Quién es la víctima?

Cálmese.

¿Que ocurrió?/¿Qué pasó?

Communication

I speak a little Spanish.

Do you speak English?

I've called for a Spanish-speaking officer.

I don't understand.

Do you understand?

How may I help you?

Let's talk in the other room.

Slowly.

Please repeat.

La comunicación

Hablo un poco de español.

¿Habla usted inglés?

Llamé a un oficial que habla español.

No entiendo./No comprendo.

¿Entiende?/¿Comprende?

¿Cómo puedo ayudarlo?

Hablemos en el otro cuarto.

Despacio.

Repita, por favor.

Traffic Questions

Name

Place of Birth

Age

Las preguntas para el tráfico

Nombre

Lugar de nacimiento

Edad

Occupation	Ocupación
Address	Dirección / Domicilio
City	Ciudad
Zip Code	Zona postal
When were you born?	¿Cuándo nació?
Phone Number	Número de teléfono
Place of Work	Lugar donde trabaja
Sign here	Firme aquí
Insurance	Seguro
Driver's License	Licencia de manejar
Are you the owner of this car?	¿Es usted el dueño de este carro?
Vehicle?	¿vehículo?
Get out of the car.	Salga del carro / Fuera del carro.
Stop the motor, please.	Apague el motor, por favor.

Accident Investigation	**La investigación del accidente**
Is anyone injured?	¿Hay alguien lastimado?
Are you all right?	¿Está bien?
Stay calm.	Cálmese.
Don't move.	No se mueva.
Where does it hurt?	¿Dónde le duele?
Do you need an ambulance?	¿Necesita una ambulancia?
I'm going to call an ambulance.	Voy a llamar una ambulancia.
Turn off the motor.	Apague el motor.
Get out of the vehicle.	Salga del vehículo.
Whose vehicle is this?	¿De quién es el vehículo?
Who was driving?	¿Quién estaba manejando?
Did you put on your seat belt?	¿Se puso el cinturón de seguridad?
Which way were you going?	¿En qué dirección iba?
How fast were you driving?	¿A qué velocidad estaba manejando?
Which way was the other vehicle going?	¿En qué dirección iba el otro vehículo?
Do you want me to call a tow truck?	¿Quiere que llame una grúa?
Do you want me to call someone?	¿Quiere que llame a alguien?
Have you been drinking or taking drugs?	¿Ha bebido alcohol o tomado drogas?

Numbers

one	uno
two	dos
three	tres
four	cuatro
five	cinco
six	seis
seven	siete
eight	ocho
nine	nueve
ten	diez
eleven	once
twelve	doce
thirteen	trece
fourteen	catorce
fifteen	quince
sixteen	diez y seis
seventeen	diez y siete
eighteen	diez y ocho
nineteen	diez y nueve
twenty	veinte
thirty	treinta
forty	cuarenta
fifty	cincuenta
sixty	sesenta
seventy	setenta
eighty	ochenta
ninety	noventa
one hundred	cien/ciento
one thousand	mil
two thousand	dos mil

Days of the Week

Monday	lunes
Tuesday	martes
Wednesday	miércoles
Thursday	jueves

Los números

Los días de la semana

Friday	viernes
Saturday	sábado
Sunday	domingo

Months of the Year / Los meses del año

January	enero
February	febrero
March	marzo
April	abril
May	mayo
June	junio
July	julio
August	agosto
September	septiembre
October	octubre
November	noviembre
December	diciembre

Time / El tiempo

What time is it?	¿Qué hora es?/¿Qué horas son?
It is one o'clock.	Es la una.
It is two o'clock.	Son las dos.
It is midday.	Es mediodía.
It is midnight.	Es medianoche.
At what time did it occur?	¿A qué hora ocurrió?
At three o'clock.	A las tres.

ARREST

The student will be proficient in common Spanish phrases that will assist the officer in assuming command and control in arrest or other police encounters.

Initial Encounter and Control / El encuentro inicial y el control

Police! Don't move.	¡Policía! No se mueva.
Drop the weapon.	Suelte el arma.
Hands in the air.	Manos arriba.
Turn around, slowly.	Voltéese despacio.
Stop!	¡Alto!
Separate your legs.	Separe las piernas.

Move and Handcuff the Suspect

Get on the floor. (inside)

Get on the ground. (outside)

Arms straight out to the side.

Cross your feet

Do not look at me.

Move to Handcuff

Give me your other hand.

Put your hands behind your back.

Commands and Arrest

Get up.

Sit down.

You are under arrest.

Mover y esposar al sospechoso

Al piso.

Al suelo.

Extienda los brazos a los lados.

Cruce los pies.

No me mire.

Mover para esposar

Deme la otra mano.

Ponga las manos detrás de la espalda.

Los mandatos y el arresto

Levántese.

Siéntese.

Está arrestado. arrestada (f)

PART I

CRIMES AGAINST PERSONS

1

Homicide/Suicide/Crowd Control

I am the police.	Soy policía.
Who called the police?	¿Quién llamó a la policía?

Personal Data Questions

What is your name?	¿Cómo se llama?
Your address?	¿Su dirección?
Daytime telephone number?	¿Su teléfono durante el día?
Nighttime telephone number?	¿Su teléfono durante la noche?
Age?	¿Su edad?
Date of birth?	¿Su fecha de nacimiento?
Where do you work?	¿Dónde trabaja?

Investigation

Who is the victim?	¿Quién es la víctima?
Where is the body?	¿Dónde está el cuerpo?
Who discovered the body?	¿Quién descubrió el cuerpo?
When did you discover the body?	¿Cuándo descubrió el cuerpo?
Did you touch the body?	¿Tocó usted el cuerpo?
Did you touch anything near the body?	¿Tocó algo cerca del cuerpo?

Did you hear any fighting?	¿Oyó a alguien peleando?
Did you hear gunshots?	¿Oyó disparos?
How many shots were fired?	¿Cuántos disparos oyó?
Did you see the attacker?	¿Vio al atacante?
Can you identify him?	¿Lo puede identificar?*
How tall is the attacker?	¿Cuánto mide el atacante?
How much does he weigh?	¿Cuánto pesa?
Where did the attacker go?	¿Adónde fue el atacante?
Did you see the weapon?	¿Vio el arma?
Did you see any vehicle?	¿Vio algún vehículo?

If the witness saw a vehicle, ask the following questions:

a. Did you notice the color of the vehicle?	a. ¿Vio el color del vehículo?
b. the brand (make) of the vehicle?	b. ¿la marca del vehículo?
c. the model of the vehicle?	c. ¿el modelo del vehículo?
d. the year of the vehicle?	d. ¿el año del vehículo?
e. the license number of the vehicle?	e. ¿el número de la placa del vehículo?
f. any visible damage on the vehicle?	f. ¿algún daño visible en el vehículo?
Are there witnesses?	¿Hay otros testigos?
Call us if you have more information.	Llámenos si tiene más información.

---

*lo = male, la = female.

II. ACTION SCENE COGNATES

victim	la víctima
attack	el ataque
the attacker	el atacante
vehicle	el vehículo
telephone	el teléfono
suicide	el suicidio
to move	mover
illegal	ilegal

III. ACTION SCENE VOCABULARY

gunshots	los disparos
witnesses	los testigos
during	durante

Verbs

to touch	tocar
Did you touch?	¿tocó?
to hear	oír
Did you hear?	¿oyó?

Interrogatives

Who?	¿Quién?
When?	¿Cuándo?
To where (what direction)?	¿Adónde?
How much?	¿Cuánto?
How many?	¿Cuántos?
What is your name?	¿Cómo se llama?
Are there witnesses?	¿Hay testigos?
Are there any other witnesses?	¿Hay otros testigos?

IV. EXPANDED VOCABULARY

body	el cadáver
to hit	pegar
murder	el asesinato
accident	el accidente
kidnapping	el secuestro
strangulation	la estrangulación

Crowd Control

Get back.	Aléjese.
Move.	Muévase.
Calm down.	Cálmese.
Your conduct is illegal.	Su conducta es ilegal.

V. ACTION SCENE STRUCTURAL EXERCISE

1. (Who)¿ _____ llamó a la policía?

2. (When)¿ _____ descubrió el cuerpo?

3. (Where)¿ _____ está el cuerpo?

4. (Did you touch)¿ _____ el cuerpo?

5. ¿Oyó (shots) _____?

6. (How many)¿ _____?

7. ¿Vio (the attacker) _____?

8. (How much) ¿ _____ mide?

9. (How much does he weigh) ¿ _____?

10. (To where) ¿ _____ fue el atacante?

11. (Are there witnesses)¿ _____?

12. (Are there other witnesses)¿ _____?

VI. ACTION SCENE QUESTIONS

1. ¿Quién llamó a la policía?

2. ¿Quién descubrió el cuerpo?

3. ¿Cuándo descubrió el cuerpo?

4. ¿Quién es la víctima?

5. ¿Tocó usted el cuerpo?

6. ¿Movió el cuerpo?

7. ¿Oyó disparos?

8. ¿Quién es el atacante?

9. ¿Adónde fue el atacante?

10. ¿Hay testigos?

11. ¿Hay otros testigos?

VII. ACTION SCENARIOS

1. You are the first officer to arrive at the home of a murdered woman.

    Her husband had called the police and he is waiting in the front yard.

    a. Identify yourself.

    ASK:

    b. Who called the police?

    c. Who is the victim?

    d. Personal Information Questions.

    e. Where is the body?

2. You are continuing with Scenario 1.

    ASK:

    a. Who discovered the body?

    b. When was the body discovered?

    c. Did you touch the body?

    d. Did you touch anything near the body?

3. A nervous neighbor has called and said that she has heard shots in the house next door.

    ASK:

    a. Did you hear anyone fighting?

    b. Did you hear gunshots?

    c. How many?

    d. Did you see the attacker?

    e. Can you identify him/her?

4. You are questioning someone who had just witnessed a murder.

    ASK:

    a. How tall is the attacker?

    b. How much does he weigh?

    c. Where did the attacker go?

    d. Did you see the weapon?

    e. Did you see any vehicle?

    If the witness saw a vehicle, ask the following questions:

Did you notice the color of the vehicle?	¿Vio el color del vehículo?
the brand (make) of the vehicle?	¿la marca del vehículo?
the model of the vehicle?	¿el modelo del vehículo?
the year of the vehicle?	¿el año del vehículo?
the license number of the vehicle?	¿el número de la placa del vehículo?
any visible damage on the vehicle?	¿algún daño visible en el vehículo?

    f. Are there witnesses?

    g. Call us if you have more information.

CHAPTER 1   HOMICIDE/SUICIDE/CROWD CONTROL: VIDEO SCRIPT

I. ACTION SCENE: INFORMANT/WITNESS/SUSPECT

Who is it?	*¿Quién es?*
I am the police.	Soy policía.
Who called the police?	¿Quién llamó a la policía?
I did.	*Yo.*

Personal Data Questions (not in video)

What is your name?	¿Cómo se llama?
Your address?	¿Su dirección?
Daytime telephone number?	¿Su teléfono durante el día?
Nighttime telephone number?	¿Su teléfono durante la noche?
Age?	¿Su edad?
Date of birth?	¿Su fecha de nacimiento?
Where do you work?	¿Dónde trabaja?

Investigation

Who is the victim?	¿Quién es la víctima?
John Smith.	*John Smith.*
Where is the body?	¿Dónde está el cuerpo?
In the room.	*En el cuarto.*
Who discovered the body?	¿Quién descubrió el cuerpo?
I did.	*Yo.*
When did you discover the body?	¿Cuándo descubrió el cuerpo?
About 5 minutes ago.	*Hace como cinco minutos.*
Did you touch the body?	¿Tocó usted el cuerpo?
No.	*No.*
Did you touch anything near the body?	¿Tocó algo cerca del cuerpo?
No. Nothing.	*No. Nada.*

Did you hear anyone fighting?	¿Oyó a alguien peleando?
Yes.	*Sí.*
Did you hear gunshots?	¿Oyó disparos?
Yes.	*Sí.*
How many shots?	¿Cuántos?
Two or three.	*Dos o tres.*
Did you see the attacker?	¿Vio al atacante?
Yes.	*Sí.*
Can you identify him?	¿Lo puede identificar?*
Yes.	*Sí.*
How tall is the attacker?	¿Cuánto mide el atacante?
About 5′ 10″.	*Como cinco pies, diez pulgadas.*
How much does he weigh?	¿Cuánto pesa?
About 160 pounds.	*Como ciento sesenta libras.*
Where did the attacker go?	¿Adónde fue el atacante?
Toward the street.	*Hacia la calle.*
Did you see the weapon?	¿Vio el arma?
No.	*No.*
Did you see any vehicle?	¿Vio algún vehículo?
Yes.	*Sí.*
The color?	¿El color?
White	*Blanco.*
The model?	¿El modelo?
Ford	*Ford.*
The year?	¿El año?
Around '92.	*Como noventa y dos.*
Are there witnesses?	¿Hay testigos?
No.	*No.*
Call us if you have more information.	Llámenos si tiene más información.

———

*lo = male, la = female.

Robbery

I. ACTION SCENE: VICTIM/WITNESS

I am the police.	Soy policía.
Are you the victim?	¿Es usted la víctima?
Are you hurt?	¿Está lastimada/o?
Who called the police?	¿Quién llamó a la policía?

Personal Data Questions

What is your name?	¿Cómo se llama?
Your address?	¿Su dirección?
Daytime telephone number?	¿Su teléfono durante el día?
Nighttime telephone number?	¿Su teléfono durante la noche?
Age?	¿Su edad?
Date of birth?	¿Su fecha de nacimiento?
Where do you work?	¿Dónde trabaja?

Investigation

What happened?	¿Qué ocurrió?
When did the robbery occur?	¿Cuándo ocurrió el robo?
Where did the robbery occur?	¿Dónde ocurrió el robo?
What was robbed?	¿Qué le robaron?

How much is each item worth?	¿Cuánto cuesta cada cosa?
How many persons robbed you?	¿Cuántas personas le robaron?
Are there witnesses?	¿Hay testigos?
Do you know the suspect?	¿Conoce al sospechoso?
Can you identify him?	¿Lo puede identificar?
Describe the suspect.	Describa al sospechoso
What did the suspect say to you?	¿Qué le dijo el sospechoso?
How long was he here?	¿Cuánto tiempo estuvo él aquí?
Was he armed?	¿Estaba armado?
Which way did he go?	¿Por dónde salió?
Call us if you have more information.	Llámenos si tiene más información.

II. ACTION SCENE COGNATES

victim	la víctima
robbery	el robo
color	el color
vehicle	el vehículo
person	la persona
armed	armado
suspect	el sospechoso
to identify	identificar
information	la información

III. ACTION SCENE VOCABULARY

Interrogatives

Who?	¿Quién?
How?	¿Cómo?
Where?	¿Dónde?
What?	¿Qué?
How many?	¿Cuantás?
How much?	¿Cuánto?
To where?	¿Por dónde?

Command Verbs

Describe the suspect.   Describa al sospechoso.

Describe the vehicle.   Describa el vehículo.

IV. EXPANDED VOCABULARY

value	el valor
credit	el crédito
identification	la identificación
property	la propiedad
personal	personal
jewelry	las joyas
cellular telephone	el teléfono celular
compact disk	el disco compacto
coin	la moneda
bicycle	la bicicleta
car	el coche / el carro
motorcycle	la motocicleta
credit card	la tarjeta de crédito
money	el dinero
purse	la bolsa
billfold	la cartera
suitcase	la maleta
radio	el radio
weapons	las armas
pistol	la pistola
club	el palo
knife	el cuchillo
switchblade	la navaja
shotgun	la escopeta
rifle	el rifle
glass	el vidrio
door	la puerta
locked	cerrado con llave
room	el cuarto
insurance	el seguro
window	la ventana
robber	el ladrón

Matching Exercise

_____	a. billfold	1. la motocicleta
_____	b. purse	2. la bolsa
_____	c. money	3. la maleta
_____	d. suitcase	4. la cartera
_____	e. jewelry	5. la ropa
_____	f. radio	6. el dinero
_____	g. clothes	7. las joyas
_____	h. motorcycle	8. el radio

V. ACTION SCENE STRUCTURAL EXERCISE

1. Soy (the police) _____.
2. ¿Es usted (the victim) _____?
3. (Are you hurt)¿ _____?
4. ¿Quién (called the police) _____?
5. ¿Qué (happened) _____?
6. ¿Cuándo (was the robbery) _____?
7. (What)¿ _____ le robaron?
8. (How many)¿ _____ personas le robaron?
9. ¿Hay (witnesses) _____?
10. Describa (the suspect) _____.
11. ¿Estaba (armed) _____?
12. ¿Lo puede (identify) _____?

VI. ACTION SCENE QUESTIONS

1. ¿Qué le robaron?
2. ¿Cuándo le robaron?
3. ¿Hay testigos?
4. ¿Estaba armado?
5. ¿Lo puede identificar?
6. ¿Por dónde salió?

▬▬ VII. ACTION SCENARIOS

1. You are investigating a robbery of a person who was walking from a shopping center and was robbed at gunpoint.

   a. Identify yourself.

   Interview the victim.

   b. Ask Personal Data Questions.

   c. What happened?

   d. When did it happen?

   e. Where did it happen?

   f. What was robbed?

   g. Call us if you have more information.

2. You are investigating a robbery of a convenience store. There was one-armed robber who stole money and cigarettes.

   Interview the clerk/victim.

   a. What happened?

   b. Where were you?

   c. What was robbed?

   d. Are there witnesses?

   e. Describe the suspect?

   f. Was he/she armed?

   g. Can you identify him/her?

   h. Call us if you have more information.

3. You are investigating a carjacking. The victim is a middle-aged male who is visiting from another state.

   Interview the victim.

   a. Are you injured?

   b. Are there witnesses?

   c. Describe the vehicle.

   If the witness saw a vehicle, ask the following questions:

   1) Did you notice the color of the vehicle?

   2) Did you notice the brand (make) of the vehicle?

   3) Did you notice the model of the vehicle?

   4) Did you notice the year of the vehicle?

5) Did you notice the license number of the vehicle?

6) Did you notice any visible damage on the vehicle?

d. Which way did the robber go?

e. Was he armed?

f. Call us if you have more information.

VIII. NOTES: WHEN DID IT HAPPEN?

When did it happen?	¿Cuándo ocurrió?
At what time?	¿A qué hora?

CHAPTER 2   ROBBERY: VIDEO SCRIPT

I. ACTION SCENE: VICTIM/WITNESS

I am the police.	Soy policía.
Are you the victim?	¿Es usted la víctima?
Yes.	*Sí.*
Are you hurt?	¿Está lastimado?
No.	*No.*
Who called the police?	¿Quién llamó a la policía?
I did.	*Yo.*

Personal Data Questions (not in video)

What is your name?	¿Cómo se llama?
Your address?	¿Su dirección?
Daytime telephone number?	¿Su teléfono durante el día?
Nighttime telephone number?	¿Su teléfono durante la noche?
Age?	¿Su edad?
Date of birth?	¿Su fecha de nacimiento?

Investigation

What happened?

A man with a pistol robbed me.

When did the robbery occur?

About 15 minutes ago.

Where did the robbery occur?

Here.

What was robbed?

A suitcase and a camera.

How much is each item worth?

The suitcase cost $500 and the camera $200.

How many persons robbed you?

One.

Are there witnesses?

No.

Do you know the suspect?

No.

Can you identify him?

Yes.

Describe the suspect.

He is a tall man with a beard.

What did the suspect say to you?

"Give me the suitcase and the camera."

How long was he here?

About two minutes.

Was he armed?

Yes, he had a pistol.

Which way did he go?

Over there.

Call us if you have more information.

¿Qué ocurrió?

Un hombre con una pistola me robó.

¿Cuándo ocurrió el robo?

Hace como unos quince minutos.

¿Dónde ocurrió el robo?

Aquí.

¿Qué le robaron?

Una maleta y una cámara.

¿Cuánto cuesta cada cosa?

La maleta cuesta quinientos y la cámara doscientos.

¿Cuántas personas le robaron?

Una.

¿Hay testigos?

No.

¿Conoce al sospechoso?

No.

¿Lo puede identificar?

Sí.

Describa al sospechoso.

Es un hombre alto y con barba.

¿Qué le dijo el sospechoso?

"Dame la maleta y la cámara."

¿Cuánto tiempo estuvo él aquí?

Como dos minutos.

¿Estaba armado?

Sí, tenía una pistola.

¿Por dónde salió?

Por allá.

Llámenos si tiene más información.

Time of the Day, Afternoon, Night	
at 6 in the morning	a las seis de la mañana
at 4 in the afternoon	a las cuatro de la tarde
at 10 at night	a las diez de la noche

When?

during the day	durante el día
during the night	durante la noche
noon	al mediodía
midnight	a medianoche
at dusk	al anochecer
at dawn	al amanecer

The Past

last year	el año pasado
last month	el mes pasado
last week	la semana pasada
last night	anoche
night before last	antenoche
day before yesterday	anteayer
3 days ago	hace 3 días
5 days ago	hace 5 días
1 week ago	hace 8 días
2 weeks ago	hace 15 días

Cultural Note: 8 days is one week and 15 days is two weeks in some Spanish speaking countries:

1 week = 8 days = ocho días

2 weeks = 15 days = quince días

Cultural Note: Time

The concept of time in Spanish speaking countries is far more open and more flexible than in other countries. In Mexico, one says, "vivo hoy en este momento," meaning "I live today in this moment."

Assault

I. ACTION SCENE: VICTIM

I am the police.	Soy policía.
Who called the police?	¿Quién llamó a la policía?
Are you injured?	¿Está lastimada/o?
Do you need an ambulance?	¿Necesita una ambulancia?
Calm down.	Cálmese.
The ambulance is on its way.	Ya viene la ambulancia.

Personal Data Questions

What is your name?	¿Cómo se llama?
Your address?	¿Su dirección?
Daytime telephone number?	¿Su teléfono durante el día?
Nighttime telephone number?	¿Su teléfono durante la noche?
Age?	¿Su edad?
Date of birth?	¿Su fecha de nacimiento?
Where do you work?	¿Dónde trabaja?

Investigation

Who hit you?	¿Quién le pegó?
Where were you struck?	¿Dónde le pegó?

When were you hit?	¿Cuándo le pegó?
What did you get hit with?	¿Con qué le pegó?
Do you want to file a criminal charge?	¿Quiere hacer una denuncia?
Did he hit anyone else?	¿Le pegó a alguien más?
Did anyone else see or hear the fight?	¿Alguien oyó o vio la pelea?
Who struck first?	¿Quién pegó primero?
Where did the suspect go?	¿Adónde fue el sospechoso?
Have you been drinking?	¿Ha tomado usted alcohol?
Has the suspect been drinking?	¿Ha tomado alcohol el sospechoso?
Taking drugs?	¿Tomado drogas?
I am going to make a report.	Voy a hacer un reporte.
Call us if you have more information.	Llámenos si tiene más información.

II. ACTION SCENE COGNATES

alcohol	el alcohol
drugs	la droga
Do you need an ambulance?	¿Necesita una ambulancia?

III. ACTION SCENE VOCABULARY

Are you hurt?	¿Está lastimada /o?
suspect	el sospechoso
to hit, strike	pegar
Who hit her/him?	¿Quién le pegó?
fight	la pelea

Interrogatives

Who?	¿Quién?
Where?	¿Dónde?
When?	¿Cuándo?
With what?	¿Con qué?
To where?	¿Adónde?

Command

Calm down.	Cálmese.

IV. EXPANDED VOCABULARY

He is wounded.	Está lastimado.
He is drunk.	Está borracho.
He is bleeding.	Está sangrando.
He shot the pistol.	Disparó la pistola.
What did he hit you with?	¿Con qué le pegó?
With . . .	¿Con . . .
hand?	la mano?
bottle?	una botella?
club?	un palo?
knife?	un cuchillo?
something else?	otra cosa?

V. ACTION SCENE STRUCTURAL EXERCISES

1. Soy (police) _____.
2. (Who) ¿ _____ llamó a la policía?
3. ¿Está (hurt) _____?
4. ¿Quién le (hit) _____?
5. (With what?) ¿ _____ le pegó?
6. ¿Dónde está (the suspect) _____?

VI. ACTION SCENARIOS

1. You are answering a police call from a young woman who has been assaulted by her boyfriend.

   a. Identify yourself.

   b. Who called the police?

   c. Are you injured?

   d. Do you need an ambulance?

   e. Calm down.

   f. The ambulance is on the way.

2. You are a police officer conducting an investigation with an elderly man who has been assaulted.

   a. Ask Personal Data Questions.

   b. Who hit you?

c. Where were you hit?

d. When were you hit?

e. What did you get hit with?

f. Where did the suspect go?

g. Have you been drinking?

h. I am going to make a report.

CHAPTER 3   ASSAULT: VIDEO SCRIPT

I. ACTION SCENE: VICTIM

I am the police.	Soy policía.
Come in.	*Pase.*
Who called the police?	¿Quién llamó a la policía?
I did.	*Yo.*
Are you injured?	¿Está lastimada?
Yes.	*Sí.*
Do you need an ambulance?	¿Necesita una ambulancia?
Calm down.	Cálmese.
The ambulance is on its way.	Ya viene la ambulancia.

Personal Data Questions

What is your name?	¿Cómo se llama?
Your address?	¿Su dirección?
Daytime telephone number?	¿Su teléfono durante el día?
Nighttime telephone number?	¿Su teléfono durante la noche?
Age?	¿Su edad?
Date of birth?	¿Su fecha de nacimiento?
Where do you work?	¿Dónde trabaja?

Investigation

Who hit you?	¿Quién le pegó?
My friend, Jessie López.	*Mi amigo, Jessie López.*
Where were you struck?	¿Dónde le pegó?
On the face.	*En la cara.*

When were you hit?

About 2 hours ago.

What did he hit you with?

With his hand.

Do you want to file a criminal charge?

Yes.

Did he hit anyone else?

No.

Did anyone else see or hear the fight?

Yes, I did.

Who struck first?

Jessie.

Where did the suspect go?

I do not know.

Have you been drinking?

A little.

Has the suspect been drinking?

Yes, a lot.

Taking drugs?

I do not believe so.

I am going to make a report.

Call us if you have more information.

Thanks.

¿Cuándo le pegó?

Hace como dos horas.

¿Con qué le pegó?

Con la mano.

¿Quiere hacer una denuncia?

Sí.

¿Le pegó a alguien más?

No.

¿Alguien oyó o vio la pelea?

Sí, yo.

¿Quién pegó primero?

Jessie.

¿Adónde fue el sospechoso?

No sé.

¿Ha tomado usted alcohol?

Un poco.

¿Ha tomado alcohol el sospechoso?

Sí, mucho.

¿Tomado drogas?

No creo.

Voy a hacer un reporte.

Llámenos si tiene más información.

Gracias.

Sexual Assault

I. ACTION SCENE: VICTIM/WITNESS INTERVIEW

I am the police.	Soy policía.
Who called the police?	¿Quién llamó a la policía?
Who is the victim?	¿Quién es la víctima?
Are you injured?	¿Está lastimada?
Calm down.	Cálmese.
Do you need help?	¿Necesita ayuda?
Do you need to go to a hospital?	¿Necesita ir al hospital?

Personal Data Questions

What is your name?	¿Cómo se llama?
Your address?	¿Su dirección?
Daytime telephone number?	¿Su teléfono durante el día?
Nightime telephone number?	¿Su teléfono durante la noche?
Age?	¿Su edad?
Date of birth?	¿Su fecha de nacimiento?
Where do you work?	¿Dónde trabaja?

Investigation

I am going to ask you some difficult questions.	Le voy a hacer unas preguntas difíciles.
When did the attack happen?	¿Cuándo fue el ataque?
Where did the attack happen?	¿Dónde fue el ataque?
Do you know the attacker?	¿Conoce al atacante?
What is his name?	¿Cómo se llama?
His address?	¿Su dirección?
What rooms did he enter?	¿A qué cuartos entró?
Where did he go?	¿Adónde fue él?
Were you alone?	¿Estaba usted sola?
Are there witnesses?	¿Hay testigos?
Did you fight?	¿Pelearon?
Did he penetrate your vagina?	¿Él penetró su vagina?
Did he have an orgasm?	¿Tuvo él una eyaculación?
Where are the clothes you were wearing?	¿Dónde está la ropa que usted llevaba?
Those clothes can be used as evidence.	Esta ropa puede ser usada como evidencia.
Describe the attacker.	Describa al atacante.
How tall is he?	¿Cuánto mide?
How much does he weigh?	¿Cuánto pesa?
How old is he?	¿Cuántos años tiene?
Call us if you have more information.	Llámenos si tiene más información.

II. ACTION SCENE COGNATES

to attack	atacar
the attacker	el atacante
police	la policía
victim	la víctima
telephone	el teléfono
hospital	el hospital
to need	necesitar
vehicle	el vehículo
evidence	la evidencia
report	el reporte
description	la descripción

III. ACTION SCENE VOCABULARY

to hit	pegar
Who hit you?	¿Quién le pegó?
to help	ayudar
Do you need help?	¿Necesita ayuda?
difficult questions	las preguntas difíciles
clothing	la ropa

Interrogatives

When?	¿Cuándo?
How much?	¿Cuánto?
How many?	¿Cuántos?
What?	¿Qué?
Who?	¿Quién?
How?	¿Cómo?
Where?	¿Dónde?
To where?	¿Adónde?

IV. EXPANDED VOCABULARY

rape	la violación
condom	el condón
AIDS	el SIDA (el síndrome de inmunodeficiencia adquirida)

V. ACTION SCENE STRUCTURAL EXERCISE

1. Soy (the police) _____.
2. ¿Quién (called) _____ la policía?
3. ¿Quién es (the victim) _____?
4. (Calm down) _____.
5. ¿Está (injured) _____?
6. (Do you need) ¿ _____ ayuda?
7. ¿Necesita ir (to the hospital) _____?

VI. ACTION SCENE QUESTIONS

1. ¿Quién es la víctima?
2. ¿Necesita ayuda?
3. ¿Necesita ir al hospital?
4. ¿Cuándo fue el ataque?
5. ¿Dónde fue el ataque?
6. ¿Pelearon?

VII. ACTION SCENARIOS

1. You are first to arrive at the scene of a sexual assault.
   a. Identify yourself.
   b. Who called the police?
   c. Who is the victim?
   d. Are you injured?
   e. Do you need help?
   f. Do you need to go to the hospital?
   g. Ask Personal Data Questions.

2. You are investigating a sexual assault. Tell the victim that you have some difficult questions to ask regarding the incident.
   a. When did the attack happen?
   b. Where did the attack happen?
   c. Do you know the attacker?
   d. What is his name?
   e. What rooms did he enter?
   f. Where did he go?
   g. Are there witnesses?

3. You are finishing an investigation in the home of a young female victim who claims to have been sexually assaulted.
   a. Describe the attacker.
   b. How tall is he?
   c. How much does he weigh?
   d. How old is he?
   e. Where are the clothes you were wearing?
   f. Call us if you have any more information.

CHAPTER 4   SEXUAL ASSAULT: VIDEO SCRIPT

I. ACTION SCENE: VICTIM/WITNESS INTERVIEW

Who is it?	*¿Quién es?*
I am the police.	Soy policía.
Come in.	*Pase.*
Who called the police?	¿Quién llamó a la policía?
I did.	*Yo.*
Who is the victim?	¿Quién es la víctima?
I am.	*Yo.*
Are you injured?	¿Está lastimada?
Yes.	*Sí.*
Calm down.	Cálmese.
Do you need help?	¿Necesita ayuda?
Yes.	*Sí.*
Do you need to go to the hospital?	¿Necesita ir al hospital?
No.	*No.*

Personal Data Questions

What is your name?	¿Cómo se llama?
Alice Solís.	*Alicia Solís.*
Your address?	¿Su dirección?
5323 12th Street.	*Cinco mil trescientos veinte y tres Calle Doce.*
Daytime telephone number?	¿Su teléfono durante el día?
582-1121.	*Cinco ochenta y dos once veinte y uno.*
Nightime telephone number?	¿Su teléfono durante la noche?
Age?	¿Su edad?
36.	*Treinta y seis.*
Date of birth?	¿Su fecha de nacimiento?
March 23, 1963.	*Veinte y tres de marzo de mil novecientos sesenta y tres.*
Where do you work?	¿Dónde trabaja?

Investigation

I am going to ask you some difficult questions.	Le voy a hacer unas preguntas difíciles.
When did the attack happen?	¿Cuándo fue el ataque?
About an hour ago.	*Hace una hora.*
Where did the attack happen?	¿Dónde fue el ataque?
Here in my house.	*Aquí en mi casa.*
Do you know the attacker?	¿Conoce al atacante?
Yes. He is an ex boyfriend.	*Sí, es un ex novio.*
What is his name?	¿Cómo se llama?
Paul Ramírez.	*Pablo Ramírez.*
His address?	¿Su dirección?
2510 5th Street.	*Dos mil quinientos diez, Calle Cinco.*
What rooms did he enter?	¿A qué cuartos entró?
The living room.	*A la sala.*
Where did he go?	¿Adónde fue él?
I do not know.	*No sé.*
Were you alone?	¿Estaba usted sola?
No.	*No.*
Are there witnesses?	¿Hay testigos?
Yes. Anita, my neighbor.	*Sí, Anita, mi vecina.*
Did you fight?	¿Pelearon?
Yes.	*Sí.*
Did he penetrate your vagina?	¿El penetró su vagina?
Yes.	*Sí.*
Did he have an orgasm?	¿Tuvo él una eyaculación?
Yes.	*Sí.*
Where are the clothes you were wearing?	¿Dónde está la ropa que usted llevaba?
In the bathroom.	*En el baño.*
These clothes can be used as evidence.	Esta ropa puede ser usada como evidencia.
Describe the attacker.	Describa al atacante.
How tall is he?	¿Cuánto mide?
About 5′ 8″.	*Como cinco pies, ocho pulgadas.*
How much does he weigh?	¿Cuánto pesa?
About 160 lbs.	*Como ciento sesenta libras.*

How old is he?	¿Cuántos años tiene?
37.	*Treinta y siete.*
Call us if you have more information.	Llámenos si tiene más información.
Thank you.	*Gracias.*

Cultural Note: Discussing Rape/Statistics on Rape

In some Spanish-speaking countries, discussing rape or parts of the female anatomy may be considered socially unacceptable. Therefore, a report of this nature may require patience, diplomacy and sensitivity.

Cultural Note

Some Spanish speaking people may be more comfortable providing height and weight in metric form. Here is an easy conversion chart you can use.

- Multiply inches by 2.54 to get centimeters (this conversion factor is **exact**)
- Multiply feet by 0.305 to get meters
- Multiply miles by 1.6 to get kilometers
- Divide pounds by 2.2 to get kilograms
- Multiply ounces by 28 to get grams
- Multiply fluid ounces by 30 to get milliliters
- Multiply gallons by 3.8 to get liters

Child Abuse

I. ACTION SCENE: INFORMANT/SUSPECT INTERVIEW

I am the police.	Soy policía.
I am a representative from the child protection service.	Soy representante del servicio de protección a niños.
We are investigating a report of child abuse.	Estamos investigando un reporte de abuso a un niño.

Personal Data Questions

What is your name?	¿Cómo se llama?
Your address?	¿Su dirección?
Daytime telephone number?	¿Su teléfono durante el día?
Nighttime telephone number?	¿Su teléfono durante la noche?
Age?	¿Su edad?
Date of birth?	¿Su fecha de nacimiento?
Where do you work?	¿Dónde trabaja?

Investigation

What is the name of the child?	¿Cómo se llama el niño?
How old is the child?	¿Cuántos años tiene?
Where is the child?	¿Dónde está el niño?

We would like to examine the child for signs of abuse.	Queremos examinar al niño para buscar las señas del maltrato en el niño.
Where is a private room?	¿Dónde hay un cuarto con privacía?

With the Suspect

What is your name?	¿Cómo se llama usted?
What is your relation to the child?	¿Cuál es su relación con el niño?
When was the child injured?	¿Cuándo se lastimó el niño?
How did the child receive injuries?	¿Cómo se lastimó el niño?
Did he fall down?	¿Se cayó?
Did he touch something hot?	¿Tocó algo caliente?
Where were you when he was injured?	¿Dónde estaba usted cuando se lastimó el niño?
Who was with him when he was injured?	¿Quién estaba cuando se lastimó?
Did you take him to the doctor?	¿Lo llevó al doctor?
Did you take him to the clinic?	¿Lo llevó a la clínica?
Did you take him to the hospital?	¿Lo llevó al hospital?
How do you correct the child?	¿Cómo corrige a su niño?
Do you hit the child?	¿Le pega al niño?
Show me how.	Enséñeme cómo.
There will be an investigation.	Habrá una investigación.

II. ACTION SCENE COGNATES

service	el servicio
protection	la protección
minors	los menores
investigating	investigando
report	el reporte
abuse	el abuso
telephone	el teléfono
examine	examinar
relation	la relación
doctor	el doctor

III. ACTION SCENE VOCABULARY

signs of abuse	señas del maltrato
to hit	pegar
Do you hit the child?	¿Le pega al niño?
to correct	corregir
How do you correct the child?	¿Cómo corrige al niño?

Interrogatives

How many?	¿Cuántos?
Where?	¿Dónde?
Which	¿Cuál? (means "What" when used before "es")
Who?	¿Quién?
What?	¿Qué?
How?	¿Cómo?

Commands

Show me.	Enséñeme.

IV. EXPANDED VOCABULARY

mad	enojado
drunk	borracho
lie	la mentira
bar	el bar

Corporal Punishment

slap	la bofetada
bite	la mordida
beating	la paliza
kick	la patada
spanking, slap in the buttocks	la nalgada
cuts	las cortadas
burns	las quemaduras
bruises	los moretones

Parts of the Body

arm	el brazo
leg	la pierna
neck	el cuello
head	la cabeza
back	la espalda
face	la cara
hand	la mano

Frequency of Time

all the time	todo el tiempo
every day	todos los días
always	siempre
frequently	frecuentemente

V. ACTION SCENE STRUCTURAL EXERCISE

1. Soy (the police) _____.
2. Estoy investigando un reporte de (abuse) _____ a un niño.
3. (Who)¿ _____ llamó a la policía?
4. Quiero (examine) _____ al niño para busca las señas del maltrato.
5. ¿(Where) _____ hay un cuarto con privacía?
6. ¿Cuál es su (relation) _____ con el niño?
7. (When)¿ _____ se lastimó el niño?
8. (How)¿ _____ se lastimó el niño?
9. ¿Llevó al niño (to the doctor) _____?
10. (Do you hit)¿ _____ al niño?
11. (Show me) _____ cómo.
12. Habrá (an investigation) _____ .

VI. ACTION SCENE QUESTIONS

1. ¿Cúantos años tiene el niño?
2. ¿Cuándo se lastimó el niño?
3. ¿Cómo se lastimó el niño?
4. ¿Lo llevaron al hospital?

▓ VII. ACTION SCENARIOS

1. You arrive at home where there is a child who has been burned.

   a. Identify yourself.

   b. Who called the police?

   c. Ask Personal Data Questions.

2. You are continuing with the investigation in Scenario 1.

   a. How old is the child?

   b. Is the child here?

   c. I want to examine the child for signs of abuse.

   d. Where is a private room?

3. You are investigating a child abuse case. The suspect is the child's uncle.

   a. What is your relation to the child?

   b. How did the child receive injuries?

   c. When was the child injured?

   d. Where was the child injured?

4. You are continuing the investigation in Scenario 3.

   a. Did you take him to the doctor?

   b. How do you correct the child?

   c. Do you hit the child?

   d. Show me how.

   e. There will be an investigation.

CHAPTER 5   CHILD ABUSE: VIDEO SCRIPT

▓ I. ACTION SCENE: INFORMANT/SUSPECT INTERVIEW

Who is it?	*¿Quién es?*
I am the police.	Soy policía.
Come in.	*Pase.*
I am a representative from the child protection service.	Soy representante del servicio de protección a niños.
Be seated.	*Tomen asiento.*
We are investigating a report of child abuse.	Estamos investigando un reporte de abuso a un niño.

Personal Data Questions (not in video)

What is your name?	¿Cómo se llama?
Your address?	¿Su dirección?
Daytime telephone number?	¿Su teléfono durante el día?
Nighttime telephone number?	¿Su teléfono durante la noche?
Age?	¿Su edad?
Date of birth?	¿Su fecha de nacimiento?
Where do you work?	¿Dónde trabaja?

Investigation

What is the name of the child?

Alexander.

How old is the child?

14.

Where is the child?

Over there.

We would like to examine the child for signs of abuse.

Where is a private room?*

In the bedroom.

¿Cómo se llama el niño?

Alejandro.

¿Cuántos años tiene?

Catorce.

¿Dónde está el niño?

Allá.

Queremos examinar al las señas del maltrato en el niño.

¿Dónde hay un cuarto con privacía?

En la recámara.

_____

*This may vary with each state law.

With the Suspect

What is your name?

Lucero Martínez.

What is your relation to the child?

I am his mother.

When was the child injured?

Last night.

How did the child receive injuries?

Did he fall down?

He fell down.

Did he touch something hot?

No.

¿Cómo se llama usted?

Lucero Martínez.

¿Cuál es su relación con el niño?

Soy su mamá.

¿Cuándo se lastimó el niño?

Anoche.

¿Cómo se lastimó el niño?

¿Se cayó?

Se cayó.

¿Tocó algo caliente?

No.

Where were you when he was injured?	¿Dónde estaba usted cuando se lastimó el niño?
Here in the house.	*Aquí en la casa.*
Who was with him when he was injured?	¿Quién estaba cuando se lastimó?
No one.	*Nadie.*
Did you take him to the doctor?	¿Lo llevó al doctor?
No.	*No.*
to the clinic?	¿a la clínica?
No.	*No.*
to the hospital?	¿Al hospital?
No.	*No.*
How do you correct the child?	¿Cómo corrige a su niño?
Do you hit the child?	¿Le pega?
Yes.	*Sí.*
Show me how.	Enséñeme cómo.
With this.	*Con esto.*
There will be an investigation.	Habrá una investigación.

Cultural Note: Families, Eye Contact

• Hispanic families are usually very close-knit.

• Children may not make eye contact with adults, as this would be possibly construed as insolence. Therefore, in some cultures, lack of eye contact is considered a sign of respect.

75% to 90% of the injured children are thought to *know* who has committed the abuse.

In Case of Abuse of Minors

a. Call the police.	a. Llame a la policía.
b. Leave home and take the children.	b. Salga de la casa y llévese a los niños.
c. Look for medical attention.	c. Busque atención médica.
d. Look for professional help.	d. Busque ayuda profesional.

Domestic Dispute

I. ACTION SCENE: INFORMANT/VICTIM INTERVIEW

I am the police.	Soy policía.
Are your hurt?	¿Está lastimada?
Do you need help?	¿Necesita ayuda?
Do you need a doctor?	¿Necesita un doctor?

Personal Data Questions

What is your name?	¿Cómo se llama?
Your address?	¿Su dirección?
Daytime telephone number?	¿Su teléfono durante el día?
Nighttime telephone number?	¿Su teléfono durante la noche?
Age?	¿Su edad?
Date of birth?	¿Su fecha de nacimiento?
Where do you work?	¿Dónde trabaja?

Investigation

Do you live here?	¿Vive aquí?
Who else is in the house?	¿Quién más está en la casa?
When were you assaulted?	¿Cuándo le pegó?
Where were you assaulted?	¿Dónde le pegó?

Who hit you?	¿Quién le pegó?
What did he hit you with?	¿Con qué le pegó?
with his hand?	¿con la mano?
with a bottle?	¿con una botella?
Did he hit anyone else?	¿Le pegó a alguien más?
Where is he now?	¿Dónde está él ahora?
Do you want to file charges?	¿Quiere hacer una denuncia?
Are there witnesses?	¿Hay testigos?
Do you want to go to a womens' shelter (refuge)?	¿Quiere ir al refugio de mujeres?

II. ACTION SCENE COGNATES

police	la policía
doctor	el doctor
spouse, husband, wife (fem.)	el esposo, la esposa
legal	legal
to need	necesitar

III. ACTION SCENE VOCABULARY

hand	la mano
to hit	pegar
now	ahora
witnesses	los testigos
hurt	lastimada
women's refuge (shelter)	el refugio de mujeres
witnesses	los testigos
Do you want to file charges?	¿Quiere hacer una denuncia?

Directions

here	aquí
over there	ahí, allá
over there (at a distance)	allí
there is, there are	hay

Interrogatives

Who?	¿Quién?
Where?	¿Dónde?
With whom?	¿Con quién?
When?	¿Cuándo?

Commands

Calm down.	Cálmese.

IV. EXPANDED VOCABULARY

mistreatment	el maltrato
abuse	el abuso
pardon	el perdón
forgive me	perdóneme
to cut	cortar
She/he is afraid	Tiene miedo
I am afraid	Tengo miedo
bar	el bar
lie	la mentira
reason	la razón
to protect oneself	protegerse

Descriptives

He/she is	Está
mad	enojado
tired	cansado
drunk	borracho
drinking, drunk	tomado
traumatized, upset	traumatizado
confused	confundido
pregnant	embarazada
hurt	lastimado
hurt, wounded	herido
nervous	nervioso
sick	enfermo, malo

The Weapon

What did he hit you with?	¿Con qué le pegó?
With	Con
fist	el puño
club, bat	el palo
knife	el cuchillo
switchblade	la navaja
bottle	la botella
glass	el vidrio
club, bat	el palo
something else?	¿otra cosa?

V. ACTION SCENE STRUCTURAL EXERCISE

1. Soy (the police) _____.
2. ¿Está (hurt) _____?
3. ¿Necesita (a doctor) _____?
4. (Who)¿ _____ llamó a la policía?
5. ¿Vive (here) _____?
6. (Who else)¿ _____ está en la casa?
7. (Calm yourself) _____.
8. ¿Quién (hit you) _____?
9. (With what)¿ _____ le pegó?
10. (Where)¿ _____ está él ahora?
11. ¿Quiere hacer (legal charges) _____?
12. ¿Quiere ir al (a refuge) _____ de mujeres?

VI. ACTION SCENE QUESTIONS

1. ¿Necesita un doctor?
2. ¿Está lastimada?
3. ¿Quién llamó a la policía?
4. ¿Dónde le pegó?
5. ¿Quién le pegó?
6. ¿Con qué le pegó?
7. ¿Dónde está él ahora?

8. ¿Quiere hacer una denuncia?

9. ¿Quiere ir al refugio de mujeres?

VII. ACTION SCENARIOS

1. You are investigating a case where the female victim claims that her husband has assaulted her.

   a. Identify yourself.

   b. Are you hurt?

   c. Do you need help?

   d. Do you need a doctor?

   e. Who called the police?

2. You are continuing the questioning of the case from Scenario 1.

   a. Ask Personal Data Questions.

   b. Do you live here?

   c. Who else is in the house?

3. You are continuing the questioning of the case from Scenario 1.

   a. When were you assaulted?

   b. Where were you assaulted?

   c. Who hit you?

   d. What did he hit you with?

   e. Did he hit anyone else?

   f. Where is he now?

   g. Do you want to go to a woman's refuge (shelter)?

Cultural Note: Machismo and Vergüenza

- Scenes of domestic violence are found in all cultures and within all socio-economic groups.

- Some family units are centered on the male as the head of the household.

- If he receives any challenge to this authority, a male may blame his wife or a male companion. In some cases, the woman is perceived as submissive, delicate, caring for home and family and non-aggressive.

- Also, a challenge may bring great shame (vergüenza) to the male; therefore, the victim may find it very difficult to escape male power and control, and then feel embarrassment.

- In some cases, a woman may not want to file charges or a restraining order because society expects her to stand by her man regardless of the present or potential verbal, emotional, or physical abuse.

CHAPTER 6   DOMESTIC DISPUTE: VIDEO SCRIPT

I. ACTION SCENE: INFORMANT/VICTIM INTERVIEW

I am the police.	Soy policía.
Are your hurt?	¿Está lastimada /o?
Yes.	*Sí.*
Do you need help?	¿Necesita ayuda?
Do you need a doctor?	¿Necesita un doctor?
Yes.	*Sí.*

Personal Data Questions

What is your name?	¿Cómo se llama?
Anita Garza de Cortés.	*Anita Garza de Cortés.*
Your address?	¿Su dirección?
569 South Baker.	*Quinientos sesenta y nueve South Baker.*
Daytime telephone number?	¿Su teléfono durante el día?
918-582-4411.	*Novecientos diez y ocho, cinco ochenta y dos cuatro, cuatro, once*
Nighttime telephone number?	¿Su teléfono durante la noche?
The same.	*Es el mismo.*
Age?	¿Su edad?
36.	*Treinta y seis.*
Date of birth?	¿Su fecha de nacimiento?
March 23, 1963.	*Veinte y tres de marzo de mil novecientos sesenta y tres.*
Where do you work?	¿Dónde trabaja?
I do not work.	*No trabajo.*

Investigation

Do you live here?	¿Vive aquí?
Yes, here.	*Sí, aquí.*
Who else is in the house?	¿Quién más está en la casa?
My children.	*Mis hijos.*

When were you assaulted?

Last night.

Where were you assaulted?

Here on the face.

Who hit you?

My husband.

What did he hit you with?

his hand?

a bottle?

With his hand.

Did he hit anyone else?

No, just me.

Where is he now?

He has probably gone to his mother's house.

Do you want to file charges?

Yes.

Are there witnesses?

No.

Do you want to go to a womens' shelter (refuge)?

Yes.

Go ahead.

¿Cuándo le pegó?

Anoche.

¿Dónde le pegó?

Aquí en la cara.

¿Quién le pegó?

Mi esposo.

¿Con qué le pegó?

¿con la mano?

¿con una botella?

Con la mano.

¿Le pegó a alguien más?

No, sólo a mí.

¿Dónde está él ahora?

Debe de haberse ido a la casa de su mama.

¿Quiere hacer una denuncia?

Sí.

¿Hay testigos?

No.

¿Quiere ir al refugio de mujeres?

Sí.

Pase.

Missing Person

I. ACTION SCENE: INTERVIEW WITH RELATIVE/FRIEND/INFORMANT

I am the police.	Soy policía.
Who called the police?	¿Quién llamó a la policía?
Calm down.	Cálmese.

Personal Data Questions

What is your name?	¿Cómo se llama?
Your address?	¿Su dirección?
Daytime telephone number?	¿Su teléfono durante el día?
Nighttime telephone number?	¿Su teléfono durante la noche?
Age?	¿Su edad?
Date of birth?	¿Su fecha de nacimiento?
Where do you work?	¿Dónde trabaja?

Investigation

Who is missing?	¿Quién está perdido?
What is his name?	¿Cómo se llama?
Since when has he/she been missing?	¿Desde cuándo se perdió?
When did you see him/her last?	¿Cuándo (lo/la) vio por última vez?

How old is he/she?	¿Cuántos años tiene?
What clothing was he/she wearing?	¿Qué ropa llevaba?
Does he/she have any medical problems?	¿Tiene problemas de salud?
Is he/she taking medicine?	¿Toma medicina?
Is he/she with any friends?	¿Está con algunos amigos?
Did he/she threaten to run away?	¿Amenazó con escaparse?
Where does (name) go frequently?	¿Adónde va con frencuencia (nombre)?
I will send a description to the police.	Voy a mandar una descripción a la policía.
Contact us if you have more information.	Llámenos si tiene más información.
Contact us if the person returns.	Llámenos si regresa la persona.

II. ACTION SCENE COGNATES

person	la persona
medicine	la medicina
information	la información
frequently	con frecuencia
to escape	escaparse

III. ACTION SCENE VOCABULARY

to be missing, to be lost	perderse
is missing, is lost	se perdió
last time (the final time)	por última vez
to have	tener
he/she has	tiene
health	la salud
to threaten	amenazar
he/she threatened	amenazó
to take	tomar
he/she takes	toma
clothing	la ropa

Commands

Call us.	Llámenos.
Calm down.	Cálmese.

Interrogatives

Who?	¿Quién?
Since when?	¿Desde cuándo?
When?	¿Cuando?
What?	¿Qué?
To where?	¿Adónde?

IV. ACTION SCENE STRUCTURAL EXERCISE

1. (What is the person's name?) ¿ _____?
2. (Since when) ¿ _____ se perdió?
3. (How old is he/she?) ¿ _____?
4. ¿Qué (clothing) _____ llevaba?
5. ¿Tiene (health problems) _____?
6. ¿Toma (medicine) _____?
7. ¿Amenazó con (to run away) _____?
8. ¿Adónde va (frequently) _____?
9. Voy a mandar (a description) _____ a la policía.
10. (Call us) _____ si tiene más información.

V. ACTION QUESTIONS

1. ¿Quién está perdido (a)?
2. ¿Desde cuándo se perdió?
3. ¿Cuándo (la, lo) vio por última vez?
4. ¿Tiene problemas de salud?
5. ¿Toma medicina?
6. ¿Amenazó con escaparse?

VI. ACTION SCENARIOS

1. You are interviewing the parents of a missing fourteen-year-old girl.

    a. Identify yourself.

    b. Ask who called the police.

    c. Ask Personal Data Questions.

2. You are investigating the disappearance of an adolescent. You are interviewing an aunt in where the missing person lives.

    a. Who is missing?

    b. What is that person's name?

    c. Since when has he/she been missing?

    d. When did you see her last?

    e. How old is he/she?

    f. What clothing was he/she wearing?

3. You are an officer answering the call of a distraught mother who claims her adult son has been missing for two days.

    a. Does he have medical problems?

    b. Is he taking any medicine?

    c. Is he with some friends?

    d. Did he threaten to run away?

    e. Where does he go frequently?

    f. I am going to send a description to the police.

    g. Call us if you have any more information.

Cultural Note: Family Ties, Cousin, and Close Family Friend
In Spanish, some words have more than one meaning. For example, in Mexico, the word "primo" means cousin. "Primo" also means any type of close friend in an extended family.

CHAPTER 7   MISSING PERSON: VIDEO SCRIPT

I. ACTION SCENE: INTERVIEW WITH RELATIVE/FRIEND/INFORMANT

Who is it?	*¿Quién es?*
I am the police.	Soy policía.

Oh, come in, come in.	*Ah, pase, pase.*
Please be seated.	*Tome asiento, por favor.*
Who called the police?	¿Quién llamó a la policía?
Calm down.	Cálmese.

Personal Data Questions (not in video)

What is your name?	¿Cómo se llama?
Your address?	¿Su dirección?
Daytime telephone number?	¿Su teléfono durante el día?
Nighttime telephone number?	¿Su teléfono durante la noche?
Age?	¿Su edad?
Date of birth?	¿Su fecha de nacimiento?
Where do you work?	¿Dónde trabaja?

Investigation

Who is missing?	¿Quién está perdido?
My father.	*Mi padre.*
What is his name?	¿Cómo se llama?
José Gómez.	*José Gómez.*
Since when has he been missing?	¿Desde cuándo se perdió?
Since last night.	*Desde anoche.*
When did you see him last?	¿Cuándo lo vio por última vez?
Well, last night.	*Pues, anoche.*
How old is he?	¿Cuántos años tiene?
86.	*Ochenta y seis.*
What clothing was he wearing?	¿Qué ropa llevaba?
Well, a blue suit with a pair of black shoes.	*Pues, un traje azul con un par de zapatos negros.*
Does he have any medical problems?	¿Tiene problemas de salud?
Yes, his heart!	*Sí, ¡el corazón!*
Is he taking medicine?	¿Toma medicina?
Yes.	*Sí.*
Is he with any friends?	¿Está con algunos amigos?
No. I do not think so.	*No, no creo.*
I do not know.	*No sé.*

Did he threaten to run away?	¿Amenazó con escaparse?
No.	*No.*
Where does (name) go frequently?	¿Adónde va con frencuencia (nombre)?
Well, to the church.	*Pues, a la iglesia.*
I will send a description to the police.	*Voy a mandar una descripción a la policía.*
Contact us if you have more information.	Llámenos si tiene más información.
Contact us if the person returns.	Llámenos si regresa la persona.
Yes.	*Sí.*

Curfew Violation/Criminal Trespass

CURFEW VIOLATION

I. ACTION SCENE: MINOR ON STREET (AFTER CURFEW)

Stop.	Alto.
I am the police.	Soy policía.
It is past the legal (curfew) hour.	Ya pasó la hora legal en la calle.
Show me your identification.	Déme su identificación.

Personal Data Questions

What is your name?	¿Cómo se llama?
Your address?	¿Su dirección?
Daytime telephone number?	¿Su teléfono durante el día?
Nighttime telephone number?	¿Su teléfono durante la noche?
Age?	¿Su edad?
Date of birth?	¿Su fecha de nacimiento?
Where do you work?	¿Dónde trabaja?

Investigation

Your conduct is against the law.	Su conducta es ilegal.
Where are your parents?	¿Dónde están sus padres?

You are being issued a citation.	Está recibiendo una notificación.
Turn around.	Voltéese.
Hands behind you.	Manos atrás.
I am going to handcuff you.	Lo voy a esposar.
We are going to the police station.	Vamos a la estación de policía.

CRIMINAL TRESPASS

I.   ACTION SCENE: WARNING/ARREST

| I am the police. | Soy policía. |
| Listen! | ¡Escuche! |

Personal Data Questions

What is your name?	¿Cómo se llama?
Your address?	¿Su dirección?
Daytime telephone number?	¿Su teléfono durante el día?
Nighttime telephone number?	¿Su teléfono durante la noche?
Age?	¿Su edad?
Date of birth?	¿Su fecha de nacimiento?
Where do you work?	¿Dónde trabaja?

Report/Investigation

Here is a warning for trespassing.	Aquí tiene un aviso por una entrada ilegal.
Leave now.	Salga ahora.
Do not come back here.	No regrese aquí.
Leave here.	Salga de aquí.

Arrest

| You are under arrest for criminal trespassing. | Está arrestado por entrar a una zona prohibida. |

II. ACTION SCENE COGNATES

trespassing, intrusion criminal	la entrada ilegal (criminal)
citation	la notificación*
police station	la estación de policía
persons	las personas
You (he, she) are under arrest	Está arrestado /a

———————

*"la multa" is commonly used for both "citation" and "fine."

III. ACTION SCENE VOCABULARY

It has already passed.	Ya pasó.
legal time (curfew)	la hora legal
on the street	en la calle
your parents	sus padres
you will receive	va a recibir
the law	la ley
here	aquí
trespass	la entrada es ilegal

Interrogatives

Where?	¿Dónde?

Commands

Listen.	Escuche.
Do not return.	No regrese.
Leave.	Váyase.

IV. EXPANDED VOCABULARY

wall   la pared

space   el espacio

You should not be here.   No debe estar aquí.

owners   los dueños

warning   el aviso

jail   la cárcel

V. ACTION SCENE STRUCTURAL EXERCISE

1. Ya pasó _____ (curfew) en la calle.

2. ¿Dónde están (your parents) _____?

3. (Where)¿ _____ están sus padres?

4. Está recibiendo una notificación por (trespassing) _____.

5. Vamos a (the police station) _____.

6. Su conducta es (illegal) _____.

7. (You are under arrest) _____.

VI. ACTION SCENE QUESTIONS

1. ¿Ya pasó la hora legal?

2. ¿Dónde están sus padres?

VII. ACTION SCENE SCENARIOS

Curfew Violation

1. You are on patrol and three juveniles are spotted in front of a convenience store. It is 2:20 a.m.

   a. Identify yourself.

   b. It is past the legal hour in the street.

   c. Give me your identification.

   d. Ask Personal Data Questions.

2. You are continuing with Scenario 1.

    a. Your conduct is illegal.

    b. Where are your parents?

    c. I am going to handcuff you.

    d. We are going to the police station.

Criminal Trespass Warning/Arrest

3. A man has been sitting on the steps of city hall for three hours.

    a. Identify yourself.

    b. Listen.

    c. Leave now.

    d. Do not come back.

    e. You are under arrest for trespassing.

CHAPTER 8   CURFEW VIOLATION: VIDEO SCRIPT

I. ACTION SCENE: MINOR ON STREET (AFTER CURFEW)

Stop.	Alto.
I am the police.	Soy policía.
It is past the legal (curfew) hour.	Ya pasó la hora legal en la calle.
Show me your identification.	Déme su identificación.

Personal Data Questions (not in video)

What is your name?	¿Cómo se llama?
Your address?	¿Su dirección?
Daytime telephone number?	¿Su teléfono durante el día?
Nighttime telephone number?	¿Su teléfono durante la noche?
Age?	¿Su edad?
Date of birth?	¿Su fecha de nacimiento?
Where do you work?	¿Dónde trabaja?

Investigation

Your conduct is against the law.	Su conducta es ilegal.
Where are your parents?	¿Dónde están sus padres?
I do not know.	*No sé.*
You are being issued a citation.	Está recibiendo una notificación.
Turn around.	Voltéese.
Hands behind you.	Manos atrás.
I am going to handcuff you.	Lo voy a esposar.
We are going to the police station.	Vamos a la estación de policía.

CHAPTER 8   CRIMINAL TRESPASS (NOT IN VIDEO)

I. ACTION SCENE: WARNING/ ARREST

I am the police.	Soy policía.
Listen!	¡Escuche!

Personal Data Questions

What is your name?	¿Cómo se llama?
Your address?	¿Su dirección?
Daytime telephone number?	¿Su teléfono durante el día?
Nighttime telephone number?	¿Su teléfono durante la noche?
Age?	¿Su edad?
Date of birth?	¿Su fecha de nacimiento?
Where do you work?	¿Dónde trabaja?

Report/Investigation

Here is a warning for trespassing.	Aquí tiene un aviso por una entrada ilegal.
Leave now.	Salga ahora.
Do not come back here.	No regrese aquí.
Leave here.	Salga de aquí.

Arrest

You are under arrest for criminal trespassing.	Está arrestado por entrar a una zona prohibida.

PART II

CRIMES AGAINST PROPERTY

Burglary

I. ACTION SCENE: WITNESS/VICTIM

I am the police.	Soy policía.
Who called the police?	¿Quién llamó a la policía?

Personal Data Questions

What is your name?	¿Cómo se llama?
Your address?	¿Su dirección?
Daytime telephone number?	¿Su teléfono durante el día?
Nighttime telephone number?	¿Su teléfono durante la noche?
Age?	¿Su edad?
Date of birth?	¿Su fecha de nacimiento?
Where do you work?	¿Dónde trabaja?

Investigation

Who was burglarized?	¿A quién le robaron?
Who discovered the burglary?	¿Quién descubrió el robo?
When was the burglary discovered?	¿Cuándo descubrió el robo?
Who is the owner of the burglarized property?	¿Quién es el dueño de la propiedad robada?
What was burglarized?	¿Qué le robaron?

What does each item cost?	¿Cuánto cuesta cada cosa?
The computer?	¿La computadora?
Do you have serial number? the model?	¿Tiene el número de serie? ¿el modelo?
Where did they enter?	¿Por dónde entraron?
How did they break in?	¿Cómo entraron?
Did the entry cause damage?	¿Causaron algún daño al entrar?
What rooms did they enter?	¿A qué cuártos entraron?
Was the house unoccupied?	¿Estaba sola la casa?
Since when?	¿Desde cuándo?
Did you see anyone?	¿Vio a alguien?
Do you suspect anyone?	¿Sospecha de alguien?
Did the suspects do anything else in the house?	¿Hicieron algo más en la casa?
Did they eat?	¿Comieron?
Did they use the restroom?	¿Entraron al baño?
Have you touched anything?	¿Ha tocado usted algo?
I am going to take fingerprints.	Voy a tomar las huellas digitales.
Are there witnesses?	¿Hay testigos?
Call us if your have more information.	Llámenos si tiene más información.

II. ACTION SCENE COGNATES

police	la policía
telephone	el teléfono
to rob, burglarize	robar
the robbery, burglary	robo
model	el modelo
color	el color
to cost	costar
to enter	entrar
to use	usar
fingerprints	las huellas digitales
information	la información
property	la propiedad

III. ACTION VOCABULARY

witnesses	los testigos
damage	el daño
serial number	el número de serie
the owner	el dueño

Interrogatives

Who?	¿Quién?
When?	¿Cuándo?
What?	¿Qué?
How much?	¿Cuánto?
Since when?	¿Desde cuándo?
Through where?	¿Por dónde?
Show me.	Enséñeme.
I am going to make a report.	Voy a escribir un reporte.

IV. EXPANDED VOCABULARY

the window	la ventana
in front of	enfrente de
in back of	detrás de
yours	suyas
upon entering	al entrar
someone	alguien
no one	nadie
the door	la puerta
to force	forzar

Commercial Property

building	el edificio
cash register	la caja
alarm	la alarma
security	la seguridad
guard	el guardia
glass	el vidrio

Burglary Tools

ladder	la escalera
rope	la soga
rock	la piedra
crowbar	la palanca
key	la llave
glasscutters	el cortavidrios
club, bat	el palo

Stolen Property

video camera	la cámara de video
compact disk	el disco compacto
jewelry	las joyas
television	la televisión
video cassette player	la videocasetera
money	el dinero
bicycle	la bicicleta
computer	la computadora
stereo	el estéreo
cellular telephone	el teléfono celular
billfold	la cartera

V. ACTION SCENE STRUCTURAL EXERCISES

1. (I am) _____ policía.
2. (Who)¿ _____ llamó a la policía?
3. ¿Vive (here) _____?
4. ¿A quién (was burglarized) _____?
5. ¿Quién (discovered) _____ el robo?
6. (When) ¿ _____ descubrió el robo?
7. (Who) ¿ _____ es el dueño de la propiedad robada?
8. (What) ¿ _____ le robaron?
9. (How much) ¿ _____ cuesta cada cosa?
10. ¿Tiene (the serial number) _____?
11. (Where) ¿ _____ entraron?
12. (How) ¿ _____ entraron?

13. ¿Causaron algún (damage) _____?

14. ¿Estaba (unoccupied) _____ la casa?

15. (Do you suspect) ¿ _____ de alguien?

16. ¿A qué (rooms) _____ entraron?

17. (Have you touched) ¿ _____ algo?

18. Voy a tomar (fingerprints) _____.

19. ¿Hay (witnesses) _____?

VI. ACTION SCENE QUESTIONS

1. ¿Quién llamó a la policía?

2. ¿Vive aquí?

3. ¿A quién le robaron?

4. ¿Quién descubrió el robo?

5. ¿Cuándo fue el robo?

6. ¿Qué le robaron?

7. ¿Por dónde entraron?

8. ¿Cuánto cuesta cada cosa?

9. ¿Estaba sola la casa?

10. ¿Desde cuándo estaba sola la casa?

VII. ACTION SCENARIOS

1. You are investigating a burglary in an apartment of an elderly couple.

   a. Identify yourself.

   b. Who called the police?

   c. Ask Personal Data Questions.

   d. Who was burglarized?

   e. Who discovered the burglary?

   f. When was the burglary discovered?

2. You are continuing with the investigation in Scenario 1.

   a. Who is the owner of the burglarized property?

   b. What was stolen?

   c. What does each item cost?

   d. Do you have the serial number?

3. You are continuing with Scenario 1.

   a. What rooms did they enter?

   b. Was the house unoccupied?

   c. Did you see anyone?

   d. Do you suspect anyone?

   e. Call us if you have more information.

CHAPTER 9   BURGLARY: VIDEO SCRIPT

I. ACTION SCENE: WITNESS/VICTIM

I am the police.	Soy policía.
Come in.	*Pase.*
Who called the police?	¿Quién llamó a la policía?
I did.	*Yo.*

Personal Data Questions (not in video)

What is your name?	¿Cómo se llama?
Anita Contreras.	*Anita Contreras.*
Your address?	¿Su dirección?
501 2nd Street.	*Quinientos uno Calle Dos.*
Daytime telephone number?	¿Su teléfono durante el día?
521-4018.	*Cinco, veinte y uno, cuarenta, diez y ocho.*
Nighttime telephone number?	¿Su teléfono durante la noche?
The same.	*El mismo.*
Age?	¿Su edad?
36 years old.	*Treinta y seis años.*
Date of birth?	¿Su fecha de nacimiento?
August 15, 1963.	*Quince de agosto de mil novecientos sesenta y tres.*
Where do you work?	¿Dónde trabaja?
At Benavides Pharmacy.	*En la farmacia Benavides.*

Investigation

Who was burglarized?

I was.

Who discovered the burglary?

I did.

When was the burglary discovered?

About 15 minutes ago.

Who is the owner of the burglarized property?

I am.

What was burglarized?

A television, a computer, a stereo.

What does each item cost?

The computer?

About $1000

about $400 the television

the stereo, about $300.

Do you have serial number?

No.

the model?

No, neither.

Where did they enter?

Through the front door.

How did they break in?

I do not know.

Did the entry cause damage?

No, none.

What rooms did they enter?

The living room.

Was the house unoccupied?

Yes.

Since when?

Since yesterday.

Did you see anyone?

No.

¿A quién le robaron?

A mí.

¿Quién descubrió el robo?

Yo.

¿Cuándo descubrió el robo?

Hace como quince minutos.

¿Quién es el dueño de la propiedad robada?

Yo.

¿Qué le robaron?

Una televisión, una computadora, y un estéreo.

¿Cuánto cuesta cada cosa?

¿La computadora?

Como . . . mil dólares, la televisón como cuatrocientos dólares y el estéreo como trescientos dólares.

¿Tiene el número de serie?

No.

¿el modelo?

No, tampoco.

¿Por dónde entraron?

Por la puerta principal.

¿Cómo entraron?

¡No sé!

¿Causaron algún daño al entrar?

No, ninguno.

¿A qué cuártos entraron?

A la sala.

¿Estaba sola la casa?

Sí.

¿Desde cuándo?

Desde ayer.

¿Vio a alguien?

No.

Do you suspect anyone?

No.

Did the suspects do anything else in the house?

No.

Did they eat food?

Did they use the restroom?

No.

Have you touched anything?

Nothing.

I am going to take fingerprints.

Thank you.

Are there witnesses?

No.

Call us if you have more information.

¿Sospecha de alguien?

No.

¿Hicieron algo más en la casa?

No.

¿Comieron?

¿Entraron al baño?

No.

¿Ha tocado usted algo?

Nada.

Voy a tomar las huellas digitales.

Gracias.

¿Hay testigos?

No.

Llámenos si tiene más información.

CHAPTER

10

Theft

I. ACTION SCENE: INFORMANT/VICTIM

I am the police.	Soy policía.
Who called the police?	¿Quién llamó a la policía?

Personal Data Questions

What is your name?	¿Cómo se llama?
Your address?	¿Su dirección?
Daytime telephone number?	¿Su teléfono durante el día?
Nighttime telephone number?	¿Su teléfono durante la noche?
Age?	¿Su edad?
Date of birth?	¿Su fecha de nacimiento?
Where do you work?	¿Dónde trabaja?

Investigation

Did you have something stolen?	¿Le robaron algo?
What was stolen?	¿Qué le robaron?
Anything else?	¿Algo más?
When were they stolen?	¿Cuándo le robaron?
Where were they stolen?	¿Dónde le robaron?
How were the item(s) stolen?	¿Cómo le robaron?

Where were you when the property was stolen?	¿Dónde estaba cuando le robaron?
Do you suspect anyone?	¿Sospecha de alguien?
Did you see anyone nearby?	¿Vio a alguien cerca?
Are there witnesses?	¿Hay testigos?
Call us if you have more information.	Llámenos si tiene más información.

II. ACTION SCENE COGNATES

to rob	robar
theft	el robo
to suspect	sospechar
information	la información

III. ACTION SCENE VOCABULARY

wristwatch or clock	el reloj
someone	alguien
witnesses	los testigos

IV. EXPANDED VOCABULARY

money	el dinero
briefcase	el portafolio
motorcycle	la motocicleta
furniture	las muebles
coins	las monedas
suitcase	la maleta
credit cards	las tarjetas de crédito
billfold	la cartera
purse	la bolsa
jewelry	las joyas
briefcase, portfolio	el portafolio
property	las propiedades
package	el paquete
bank	el banco
bicycle	la bicicleta

V. ACTION SCENE STRUCTURAL EXERCISE

1. (What was stolen) ¿ _____?

2. (Where were they stolen) ¿ _____?

3. (How were they stolen) ¿ _____?

4. (Where were you) ¿ _____ cuando le robaron?

5. (Do you suspect) ¿ _____ de alguien?

6. (Are there witnesses) ¿ _____?

VI. ACTION SCENARIOS

1. You are dispatched to the city library to take a theft report for a young woman.

   a. Identify yourself.

   b. Ask who called the police.

   c. Ask Personal Data Questions.

2. Continue with the Investigation questions.

   a. Did you have something stolen?

   b. What was stolen? (Option: Mention items)

   c. Anything else?

   d. When were they stolen?

   e. Where were they stolen?

   f. How were they stolen?

   g. Where were you when the property was stolen?

3. Finish the Investigation same questions.

   a. Do you suspect anyone?

   b. Did you see anyone nearby?

   c. Are there witnesses?

   d. Call us if you have more information.

CHAPTER 10 THEFT: VIDEO SCRIPT

I. ACTION SCENE: INFORMANT/VICTIM

I am the police.	Soy policía.
Who called the police?	¿Quién llamó a la policía?
I did.	*Yo.*

Personal Data Questions

What is your name?	¿Cómo se llama?
Cristina González.	*Cristina González.*
Your address?	¿Su dirección?
720 McAllen Street.	*Siete veinte Calle McAllen.*
Daytime telephone number?	¿Su teléfono durante el día?
880-3618, or	*Ocho, ochenta, treinta y seis diez y ocho.*
425-2852.	*Cuatro veinte y cinco, Veinte y ocho, cincuenta y dos.*
Nighttime telephone number?	¿Su teléfono durante la noche?
428-9356.	*Cuatro veinte y ocho, noventa y tres, cincuenta y seis.*
Age?	¿Su edad?
16.	*Diez y seis.*
Date of birth?	¿Su fecha de nacimiento?
July 3, 1984.	*El tres de julio de mil novecientos ochenta y cuatro.*
Where do you work?	¿Dónde trabaja?
At the "Downtown Store."	*En la tienda "El Centro."*

Investigation

Did you have something stolen?	¿Le robaron algo?
What was stolen?	¿Qué le robaron?
My briefcase.	*Mi portafolio.*
Anything else?	¿Algo más?
No.	*No.*
When were they stolen?	¿Cuándo le robaron?
About 10 minutes ago.	*Hace diez minutos.*
Where were they stolen?	¿Dónde le robaron?
Here.	*Aquí.*
Where were you when the property was stolen?	¿Dónde estaba cuando le robaron?
In a store.	*En una tienda.*
Do you suspect anyone?	¿Sospecha de alguien?
No.	*No.*

Did you see anyone nearby?	¿Vio a alguien cerca?
No.	*No.*
Are there witnesses?	¿Hay testigos?
I do not know.	*No sé.*
Call us if you have more information.	Llámenos si tiene más información.

Motor Vehicle Theft

I. ACTION SCENE: INFORMANT/ VICTIM

I am the police.	Soy policía.
Who called the police?	¿Quién llamó a la policía?

Personal Data Questions

What is your name?	¿Cómo se llama?
Your address?	¿Su dirección?
Daytime telephone number?	¿Su teléfono durante el día?
Nighttime telephone number?	¿Su teléfono durante la noche?
Age?	¿Su edad?
Date of birth?	¿Su fecha de nacimiento?
Where do you work?	¿Dónde trabaja?

Investigation

Who is the owner of the stolen vehicle?	¿De quién es el vehículo robado?
Describe the vehicle.	Describa el vehículo.
the color?	¿el color?
the brand? (make)	¿la marca?
the model?	¿el modelo?
the year?	¿el año?

Any visible damage?	¿Algún daño visible?
The license plate number?	¿El número de la placa?
Who saw it last?	¿Quién vio por última vez el vehículo?
When was that?	¿Cuándo fue eso?
Who discovered that it was missing?	¿Quién descubrió que no estaba?
When was it discovered missing?	¿Cuándo descubrió que no estaba?
Where was it parked?	¿Dónde estaba estacionado?
Does anyone else have the keys?	¿Alguien más tiene las llaves?
Is the vehicle paid for?	¿Está pagado el vehículo?
Do you have insurance?	¿Tiene seguro?
With whom?	¿Con quién?
I am going to make a report.	Voy a hacer un reporte.
Call us if you have more information.	Llámenos si tiene más información.

II. ACTION SCENE COGNATES

burglary, theft	el robo
color	el color
brand, make	la marca
model	el modelo
year	el año
visible	visible
number	el número
insurance	el seguro
report	el reporte
office	la oficina
vehicle	el vehículo
parked	estacionado
license plates	las placas
telephone	el teléfono

III. ACTION SCENE VOCABULARY

to find	encontrar
the last time	por última vez
the keys	las llaves
someone	alguien

Interrogatives

Who?	¿Quién?
Whose?	¿De quién?
When?	¿Cuándo?
Where?	¿Dónde?
With whom?	¿Con quién?

Command Verbs

Call us.	Llámenos.
Tell me.	Dígame.

IV. EXPANDED VOCABULARY

insurance policy	la póliza
no one	nadie
car	el coche/el carro
automobile	el automóvil
door	la puerta
locked	cerrado /a or cerrado con llave
in front of	en frente de
behind	detrás de
installment	el plazo
paid	pagado
payments	los pagos

Colors

black	negro
brown	café
blue	azul
orange	anaranjado
grey	gris
green	verde
red	rojo, colorado
yellow	amarillo
white	blanco

V. ACTION SCENE STRUCTURAL EXERCISE

1. Soy (the police) _____.

2. ¿Quién (called) _____ a la policía?

3. ¿De quién es el vehículo (stolen) _____?

4. Describa el vehículo:

    (the color) ¿_____?

    (the make) ¿_____?

    (the model) ¿_____?

    (the year) ¿_____?

    (the license number) ¿_____?

    (some visible damage)¿_____?

5. ¿Quién lo vio (the last time) _____?

6. (When was that) ¿_____?

7. ¿Alguien más tiene (the keys) _____?

8. (Is the vehicle paid for) ¿_____?

9. ¿Tiene (insurance) _____?

VI. ACTION SCENE QUESTIONS

1. ¿Está pagado el vehículo?

2. ¿Tiene seguro?

3. ¿Quién vio por última vez el vehículo?

Matching

_____ 1. el seguro	a. license plates	
_____ 2. la póliza	b. keys	
_____ 3. robado	c. insurance	
_____ 4. estacionado	d. visible damage	
_____ 5. el año	e. robbed	
_____ 6. las placas	f. policy	
_____ 7. el daño visible	g. make/brand	
_____ 8. la marca	i. parked	
_____ 9. las llaves	j. year	

VII. ACTION SCENARIOS

1. You are an officer speaking to a person who has just reported that his vehicle has been stolen.

   a. Identify yourself.

   b. Ask who called the police.

   c. Ask the Personal Data Questions.

2. Continue the questioning in Scenario 1.

   a. Who is the owner of the stolen vehicle?

   b. Describe the vehicle.

      What is the color?

      What is the make/brand?

      What is the model?

      What is the year?

      What is the license plate number?

      Is there any visible damage?

3. You are an officer investigating a stolen vehicle at a shopping center.

   a. Who saw it last?

   b. When was that?

   c. Who discovered it was missing?

   d. Where was it parked?

   e. Did someone else have the keys?

4. Continue with the questioning.

   a. Is the vehicle paid for?

   b. Do you have insurance?

   c. With whom?

   d. Call us if you have more information.

CHAPTER 11   MOTOR VEHICLE THEFT: VIDEO SCRIPT

I. ACTION SCENE: INFORMANT/ VICTIM

I am the police.	Soy policía.
Who called the police?	¿Quién llamó a la policía?
I did.	*Yo.*

Personal Data Informations

What is your name?	¿Cómo se llama?
Eva Villa Gómez.	*Eva Villa Gómez.*
Your address?	¿Su dirección?
56 Fifth Street.	*Cincuenta y seis, Calle cinco.*
Daytime telephone number?	¿Su teléfono durante el día?
428-9355.	*Cuatro veinte y ocho, noventa y tres, cincuenta y cinco.*
Nighttime telephone number?	¿Su teléfono durante la noche?
428-8493.	*Cuatro veinte y ocho, ochenta y cuatro, noventa y tres.*
Age?	¿Su edad?
I am 21 years old.	*Tengo veintiún años.*
Date of birth?	¿Su fecha de nacimiento?
January 12, 1968.	*Doce de enero del de mil novecientos sesenta y ocho.*
Where do you work?	¿Dónde trabaja?
At Gutiérrez School.	*En la escuela Gutiérrez.*

Investigation

Who is the owner of the stolen vehicle?	¿De quién es el vehículo robado?
It is mine.	*Mío.*
Describe the vehicle.	Describa el vehículo.
the color?	¿el color?
White	*Blanco.*
the brand? (make)	¿la marca?
Ford	*Ford.*
the model?	¿el modelo?
It is a Crown Victoria.	*Es un Crown Victoria.*
the year?	¿el año?
'98.	*Noventa y ocho.*
The license plate number	¿el número de la placa?
GTB-677	*GTB-seis, siete, siete.*
Any visible damage?	¿algún daño visible?
No.	*No.*

Who saw it last?	¿Quién vio por última vez el vehículo?
My father.	*Mi papá.*
When was that?	¿Cuándo fue eso?
Last night.	*Anoche.*
Who discovered that it was missing?	¿Quién descubrió que no estaba?
I did.	*Yo.*
When was it discovered missing?	¿Cuándo descubrió que no estaba?
At 8 a.m.	*A las ocho de la mañana.*
Where was it parked?	¿Dónde estaba estacionado?
Here.	*Aquí.*
Does anyone else have the keys?	¿Alguien más tiene las llaves?
No.	*No.*
Is the vehicle paid for?	¿Está pagado el vehículo?
Yes.	*Sí.*
Do you have insurance?	¿Tiene seguro?
Yes.	*Sí.*
With whom?	¿Con quién?
With America National.	*Con América Nacional.*
I am going to make a report.	Voy a hacer un reporte.
Call us if you have more information.	Llámenos si tiene más información.

Cultural Note: Automobile Insurance
Automobile insurance is voluntary in some Spanish-speaking countries.

Criminal Mischief: Vandalism

I am the police.	Soy policía.
Who called the police?	¿Quién llamó a la policía?

Personal Data Questions

What is your name?	¿Cómo se llama?
Your address?	¿Su dirección?
Daytime telephone number?	¿Su teléfono durante el día?
Nighttime telephone number?	¿Su teléfono durante la noche?
Age?	¿Su edad?
Date of birth?	¿Su fecha de nacimiento?
Where do you work?	¿Dónde trabaja?

Investigation

When was the damage discovered?	¿Cuándo descubrió el daño?
Who discovered the damage?	¿Quién descubrió el daño?
How much will it cost to repair the property?	¿Cuánto costará reparar la propiedad?
Do you suspect anyone?	¿Sospecha de alguien?
Who?	¿De quién?

Where does he/she live?	¿Dónde vive?
Are there witnesses?	¿Hay testigos?
I will write a report.	Voy a escribir un reporte.
Call us if you have more questions or more information.	Llámenos si tiene más preguntas o más información.

II. ACTION SCENE COGNATES

police	la policía
telephone	el teléfono
to discover	descubrir
Who discovered?	¿Quién descubrió?
to cost	costar
How much does it cost?	¿Cuánto cuesta?

III. ACTION SCENE VOCABULARY

the damage	el daño
to suspect	sospechar
someone	alguien
witnesses	los testigos
there is, there are	hay

Interrogatives

Who?	¿Quién?
What is (your his, her) name?	¿Cómo se llama?
When?	¿Cuándo?
How much?	¿Cuánto?
Whose?	¿De quién?
Where?	¿Dónde?

Command

| Call us. | Llámenos. |

▰▰▰▰ IV. ACTION SCENE STRUCTURAL EXERCISE

1. (Who) ¿ _____ descubrió el daño?

2. ¿Sospecha de (someone) _____?

3. (Where) ¿ _____ vive?

4. ¿Hay (witnesses) _____?

▰▰▰▰ V. ACTION SCENE SCENARIOS

1. You have been called to speak with an elderly man who is the owner of a recently vandalized vacant building.

   a. Identify yourself.

   b. Ask Personal Data Questions.

   c. Who discovered the damage?

   d. How much will it cost to repair the property?

2. You are interviewing an informant who says that her rent house has been vandalized.

   a. Do you suspect anyone?

   b. If so, who?

   c. Where does he live?

   d. Are there witnesses?

   e. I am going to write a report.

   f. Call us if you have more questions or information.

CHAPTER 12   CRIMINAL MISCHIEF: VANDALISM: VIDEO SCRIPT

▰▰▰▰ I. ACTION SCENE: INFORMANT/VICTIM

I am the police.	Soy policía.
Who called the police?	¿Quién llamó a la policía?
I did.	*Yo.*

Personal Data Questions

What is your name?	¿Cómo se llama?
Blanca Contreras.	*Blanca Contreras.*
Your address?	¿Su dirección?
511 11th Street.	*Quinientos once. Calle once.*

Daytime telephone number?	¿Su teléfono durante el día?
582-2411.	*Cinco ochenta y dos veinte y cuatro, once.*
Nighttime telephone number?	¿Su teléfono durante la noche?
It is the same.	*Es el mismo.*
Age?	¿Su edad?
30 years old.	*Treinta años.*
Date of birth?	¿Su fecha de nacimiento?
May 23, 1969.	*Veinte y trés de mayo de mil novecientos sesenta y nueve.*
Where do you work?	¿Dónde trabaja?
At the Bank of Oklahoma.	*En el banco de Oklahoma.*

Investigation

When was the damage discovered?	¿Cuándo descubrió el daño?
This morning.	*Hoy en la mañana.*
Who discovered the damage?	¿Quién descubrió el daño?
I did.	*Yo.*
How much will it cost to repair the property?	¿Cuánto costará reparar la propiedad?
About $100.	*Como unos cien dólares.*
Do you suspect anyone?	¿Sospecha de alguien?
Yes.	*Sí.*
If so, who?	¿De quién?
My neighbor.	*De mi vecino.*
Where does he/she live?	¿Dónde vive?
Here, next door.	*Aquí, al lado.*
Are there witnesses?	¿Hay testigos?
No.	*No.*
I will write a report.	Voy a escribir un reporte.
Call us if you have more questions or more information.	Llámenos si tiene más preguntas o más información.
That is fine, thank you.	*Está bien, gracias.*

PART III

TRAFFIC ENCOUNTERS

13

Driving While Intoxicated/Driving Under The Influence

I. ACTION SCENE: INTERVIEW

I am the police.	Soy la policía.
Step out of the vehicle.	Salga del vehículo.
You were stopped for not driving in a straight line.	Fue detenida por no manejar en línea recta.
Show me	Enséñeme
your driver's license,	su licencia de manejar,
your car registration,	sus papeles del registro,
your insurance papers.	sus papeles del seguro.

Investigation

Are you taking medicine?	¿Toma medicina?
What for?	¿Para qué?
At what time did you take medicine last?	¿A qué hora tomó la medicina?
Have you been drinking alcohol?	¿Ha tomado alcohol?
How many drinks did you have?	¿Cuántas bebidas alcohólicas tomó?
How long ago did you start drinking?	¿A qué hora empezó a tomar?
When was your last drink?	¿A qué hora tomó la última bebida alcohólica?

Have you smoked marijuana?	¿Ha fumado marijuana?
Are you on any other drugs?	¿Toma otra droga?
Where are you right now?	¿Dónde está ahora?
What time is it?	¿Qué hora es?
I am going to give you an alcohol test.	Voy a hacerle una prueba de alcohol.
You are under arrest.	Está arrestado.
Your car will be detained.	Su coche será detenido.

II. ACTION SCENE COGNATES

line	línea
problem	el problema
vehicle	el vehículo
license	la licencia
registration	el registro
medicine	la medicina
drug	la droga
alcohol	el alcohol

III. ACTION SCENE VOCABULARY

straight	recta
straight line	la línea recta
to drive	manejar
papers	los papeles
registration papers	los papeles de registro
to take, to drink, to consume	tomar
Do you take medicine?	¿Toma medicina?
to smoke	fumar
Have you smoked?	¿Ha fumado?
sobriety test	la prueba de alcohol
another, other	otro
now	ahora

Interrogatives

At what time?	¿A qué hora?
What time is it?	¿Qué hora es?
How many?	¿Cuántas?
Where?	¿Dónde?
Why?	¿Por qué?
because	porque

Commands

Show me . . .	Enséñeme . . .
Give me . . .	Déme . . .
Get out.	Salga.
Turn off the engine.	Apague el motor.

IV. EXPANDED VOCABULARY

highway	la carretera
road	el camino
sidewalk	la banqueta, la acera
finger	el dedo
nose	la nariz
security, insurance	el seguro

Adjectives

he/she is	Está
drunk	borracho/a
drinking	tomado
on drugs	drogado
sick	enfermo/a, malo/a

V. ACTION SCENE STRUCTURAL EXERCISE

1. (Turn off) _____ the motor.

2. (Show me) _____ su licencia.

3. (Are you taking) ¿_____ medicina?

4. (At what time) ¿_____ tomó la medicina?

5. ¿Cuántas (drinks) _____ tomó?

6. ¿ (Have you smoked) _____ marijuana?

7. ¿Toma (other) _____ drogas?

8. ¿(Where) _____ está ahora?

VI. ACTION SCENE QUESTIONS

1. ¿Toma medicina?

2. ¿A qué hora tomó la medicina?

3. ¿Ha fumado marijuana?

4. ¿Toma otra droga?

5. ¿Dónde está ahora?

6. ¿Qué hora es?

VII. ACTION SCENARIOS

1. While on patrol, you suspect a young driver is intoxicated after observing his actions. You stop the driver.

   a. Identify yourself.

   b. Step out of the vehicle.

   c. You were stopped for not driving in a straight line.

   d. Give me your license.

   e. Show me your driver's license.

   f. Show me your registration papers.

   g. Show me your insurance papers.

2. You are continuing with Scenario 1.

   a. Are you taking medicine?

   b. What for?

   c. When did you take medicine last?

   d. Have you been drinking alcohol?

   e. How many drinks did you have?

3. You have stopped a person who has been driving on the wrong side of road.

   a. Have you smoked marijuana?

   b. Are you on other drugs?

   c. Where are you now?

   d. What time is it?

   4. You are continuing with Scenario 1.

      a. I am going to give you an alcohol/drug test.

      b. Administer one of the Field Tests.

      c. You are under arrest for driving while intoxicated.

      d. Your car will be detained.

CHAPTER 13   DRIVING WHILE INTOXICATED/ DRIVING UNDER THE INFLUENCE: VIDEO SCRIPT

I. ACTION SCENE: INTERVIEW

I am the police.	Soy la policía.
Step out of the vehicle	Salga del vehículo.
You were stopped for	Fue detenida por
not driving in a straight line.	no manejar en línea recta.
Show me	Enséñeme
your driver's license,	su licencia de manejar,
your car registration,	sus papeles del registro,
your insurance papers.	sus papeles del seguro.

Investigation

Are you taking medicine?	¿Toma medicina?
Yes.	*Sí.*
What for?	¿Para qué?
For a stomach problem.	*Para un problema del estómago.*
At what time did you take medicine last?	¿A qué hora tomó la medicina?
About 2 p.m.	*Como a las dos de la tarde.*
Have you been drinking alcohol?	¿Ha tomado alcohol?
A little.	*Un poquito.*
How many drinks did you have?	¿Cuántas bebidas alcohólicas tomó?
Two.	*Dos.*
How long ago did you start drinking?	¿A qué hora empezó a tomar?
Mmm, about (pause) in the afternoon.	*Mmm... como a las... por la tarde.*
When was your last drink?	¿A qué hora tomó la última bebida alcohólica?
About 5.	*Como a las cinco.*

Have you smoked marijuana?	¿Ha fumado marijuana?
No, no.	*No, no.*
Are you on any other drugs?	¿Toma otra droga?
No.	*No.*
Where are you right now?	¿Dónde está ahora?
On Main Street.	*En la calle principal.*
What time is it now?	¿Qué hora es?
I do not know!	*¡No sé!*
I am going to give you an alcohol test.	Voy a hacerle una prueba de alcohol.
Ok.	*Ok.*
You are under arrest.	Está arrestada.
Your car will be detained.	Su coche será detenido.

FIELD TEST #1

Horizontal Gaze Nystagmus (HGN)

Remove your sunglasses.	Quítese los lentes.
Are you wearing contact lenses?	¿Usa lentes de contacto?
Look at the top of my pen.	Mire la punta de mi pluma.
Can you see my pen?	¿Puede ver mi pluma?
Follow the instrument with your eyes.	Siga el instrumento con sus ojos.
Do not move your head.	No mueva la cabeza.
I will repeat the test.	Voy a repetir la prueba.
Do the test.	Haga la prueba.

FIELD TEST #2

Finger to Nose

Stand straight.	Párese derecho/a.
Put your feet together.	Ponga sus pies juntos.
I will demonstrate for you.	Voy a demostrarle la prueba.
Extend your arms.	Extienda sus brazos.
Look up.	Mire hacia arriba.
Touch your nose with a finger. of your right hand.	Toque la nariz con el dedo de la mano derecha.
Touch your nose with a finger of your left hand.	Toque la nariz con el dedo de la mano izquierda.
Do you have any questions?	¿Tiene preguntas?
Close your eyes.	Cierre los ojos.
Do the test.	Haga la prueba.

FIELD TEST #3

One Leg Stand

Stand erect.	Párese derecho.
Put your arms to the side.	Ponga sus brazos a los lados.
I will demonstrate for you.	Se lo voy a demostrar.
Raise your (right, left) leg	Levante su pierna (derecha,
About 6 inches	izquierda) como 6 pulgadas
and count from 1 to 30	y cuente del 1 hasta 30.
Do you have questions?	¿Tiene preguntas?
Do the test.	Haga la prueba.

FIELD TEST #4

Walking Test: Heel to Toe

Do you have a problem with your back?	¿Tiene algún problema en su espalda?
with your legs?	¿en sus piernas?
with your feet?	¿en sus pies?
Take (4,5,6,7) steps one foot in front of the other.	Dé (4,5,6,7) pasos con un pie detrás del otro.
When you have taken the last step pivot on your (right, left) foot back heel to toe.	Cuando dé el último paso, voltéese en su pie (izquierdo, derecho).
Walk (4,5,6,7) steps back heel to toe.	Regrese (4,5,6,7) pasos con un pie detrás del otro.
Walk in a straight line.	Camine en línea recta.
Keep your hands and arms to your side.	Mantenga sus manos y sus brazos a los lados.
Do not hold on to yourself.	Manténgase erguido/derecho.
Do not hold on to other objects to balance.	No se recargue en nada.
Count as you take each step.	Cuente cada paso.
I will demonstrate for you.	Voy a demostrarle.
Do you have any questions?	¿Tiene preguntas?
Do the test.	Haga la prueba.

Cultural note: *Sobriety Test*

In some Spanish-speaking countries, the police do not have the authority to administer a sobriety test. A physician or technician may administer any type of test of this nature in a clinic or hospital.

C H A P T E R

14

Traffic Stop (Low Risk)

I. ACTION SCENE/INTERVIEW

I am the police.	Soy policía.
Do you have an emergency?	¿Tiene una emergencia?
Give me your driver's license,* your insurance papers and your registration papers	Déme su licencia de manejar,* sus papeles del seguro y sus papeles del registro.
Step out of the vehicle.	Salga del vehículo.
Close the door.	Cierre la puerta.
Take your hands out of your pockets.	Saque sus manos de los bolsillos.
Who is the owner of this vehicle?	¿De quién es el vehículo?
The year?	¿Qué año?
The brand?	¿Qué marca?

*"Enséñeme" which means "show me" may be used.

Citation or Warning

You are going to receive notification of an infraction for speeding.	Va a recibir una notificación de una infracción por exceso de velocidad.
Sign here.	Firme aquí.
You are not admitting your guilt.	No está admitiendo su culpabilidad.
This is a promise to contact the judge within the time allowed.	Su firma es una promesa de que va a comunicarse con el juez durante el tiempo indicado.
Be careful.	Tenga cuidado.

II. ACTION SCENE COGNATES

police	la policía
emergency	la emergencia
license	la licencia
vehicle	el vehículo
excess	el exceso
velocity, speed	la velocidad
inspection	la inspección
notification (citation)*	la notificación, el citatorio
infraction	la infracción

*"La multa" = non-standard word used in some areas for "citation"
 "La multa" = standard Spanish means "the fine"

III. ACTION VOCABULARY

vehicle	el vehículo
car	el coche, el carro
blame	la culpa
papers	los papeles
expired	vencido

Interrogative

Whose?	¿De quién?

Commands

Signature	Firme.
Give me . . .	Deme . . .

IV. EXPANDED VOCABULARY

You are going to receive a warning for	Va a recibir un aviso por
an expired inspection sticker.	un sello de inpección vencido.
an expired license.	una licencia vencida.
expired license plates.	las placas vencidas.
expired registration papers.	los papeles del registro vencidos.

illegal turn	una vuelta ilegal
light	la luz
highway	la carretera
court	la corte/el tribunal

Vehicle

light	la luz
light	el foco
front light	la luz delantera
back light	la luz trasera
glove compartment	la guantera
trunk	la cajuela
door	la puerta
battery	la batería
brakes	los frenos
tire	la llanta
windshield	el parabrisas
seat	el asiento
keys	las llaves
wheel	la llanta
window	la ventana
glass	el vidrio
steering wheel	el volante

Traffic Vocabulary

avenue	la avenida
freeway	la autopista
lane	el carril
patrol	la patrulla
collision/accident	el choque
straight ahead	derecho
to the left/on the left	a la izquierda
to the right/on the right	a la derecha
gasoline	la gasolina
zone	la zona
residential	residencial

V. ACTION SCENE STRUCTURAL EXERCISE

1. Soy (the police) _____.

2. Deme su (license) _____ de manejar, por favor.

3. Deme sus papeles del (insurance) _____.

4. ¿De quién es (the vehicle) _____?

5. (Sign) _____ (here) por favor.

VI. ACTION SCENE QUESTIONS

1. ¿Tiene una emergencia?

2. ¿De quién es el vehículo?

VII. ACTION SCENARIOS

1. You are an officer stopping a young man who has been speeding.

   a. Identify yourself.

   b. Do you have an emergency?

   c. Give me your driver's license.

   d. Give me your insurance papers.

   e. Give me your registration papers.

2. You are continuing Scenario 1.

   a. Step out of the vehicle.

   b. Close the door.

   c. Take your hands out of your pockets.

   d. Whose vehicle is this?

   e. What year?

   f. What brand?

3. You are continuing with Scenario 2.

   a. You are going to receive a notification of an infraction . . .

      1. for speeding.

      2. for an expired inspection sticker.

      3. for an expired license.

      4. for expired registration papers.

   b. Sign here.

   c. You are not admitting your guilt. This is a promise that you will contact the judge within the time allowed.

   d. Be careful.

CHAPTER 14 TRAFFIC STOP (LOW RISK): VIDEO SCRIPT

I. ACTION SCENE/INTERVIEW

I am the police.	Soy policía.
Do you have an emergency?	¿Tiene una emergencia?
No.	*No.*
Give me your driver's license,*	Déme su licencia de manejar,*
your insurance papers and	sus papeles del seguro y
your registration papers.	sus papeles del registro.
Step out of the vehicle.	Salga del vehículo.
Close the door.	Cierre la puerta.
Take your hands out of your pockets.	Saque sus manos de los bolsillos.
Who is the owner of this vehicle?	¿De quién es el vehículo?
Mine.	*Mío.*
The year?	¿Qué año?
'79	*Setenta y nueve.*
The brand?	¿Qué marca?
Chevy	*Chevy.*

___

*"Enséñeme" which means "show me" may be used.

Citation or Warning

You are going to receive notification of an infraction for speeding.	Va a recibir una notificación de una infracción por exceso de velocidad.
Sign here.	Firme aquí.
You are not admitting guilt.	No está admitiendo su culpabilidad.
This is a promise to contact the judge within the time allowed.	Su firma es una promesa de que va a comunicarse con el juez durante el tiempo indicado.
Be careful.	Tenga cuidado.

CHAPTER

15

Traffic Accident

I. ACTION SCENE: INJURED VICTIMS

I am the police.	Soy policía.
Is anyone else in the vehicle?	¿Hay alguien más en el vehículo?
Where do you hurt?	¿Dónde le duele?
Do you hurt when you move?	¿Le duele cuando se mueve?
I am going to apply this.	Voy a ponerle esto.
Do not move.	No se mueva.
Tell me if it hurts you.	Dígame si le duele.
Calm down.	Cálmese.
The ambulance is on the way.	Ya viene la ambulancia.

Action Scene: Uninjured Victims

Are you the driver of the car?	¿Es usted el conductor del vehículo?
Are you/anyone injured?	¿Está lastimado?
Is anyone else in your vehicle?	¿Hay alguien más en el vehículo?

Investigation

Show me . . .	Enséñeme . . .
your driver's license.	su licencia de manejar.
your insurance papers.	sus papeles del seguro.
car registration papers.	sus papeles del registro.

Is the information correct on your license?	¿Es correcta la información en su licencia?
Your address?	¿Su dirección?
Your telephone number?	¿Su teléfono?
Where do you work?	¿Dónde trabaja?
Who was driving the vehicle?	¿Quién estaba manejando el vehículo?
At what time did the accident occur?	¿A qué hora ocurrió el accidente?
Was it raining?	¿Llovía?
What street were you on?	¿En qué calle estaba?
Where were you going?	¿Adónde iba?
Were you trying to turn to the right?	¿Estaba tratando de doblar a la derecha?
Did you signal the turn?	¿Hizo alguna señal?
Where did the other vehicle come from?	¿De dónde venía el otro vehículo?
How fast were you going?	¿A qué velocidad iba?
Was the traffic light . . .	¿El semáforo estaba . . .
red?	rojo?
yellow?	amarillo?
green?	verde?
Did you stop?	¿Se detuvo?
Did the other vehicle stop?	¿Se detuvo el otro vehículo?
Was there a mechanical problem?	¿Había un problema mecánico en su vehículo?
Were you wearing your seat belt?	¿Se puso el cinturón de seguridad?

Moving the Vehicle

Is it possible to drive the vehicle?	¿Es posible manejar su vehículo?
A tow truck is coming.	Ya viene la grúa.
Do not move.	No se mueva.
You are receiving a (citation) notificación for an infraction.	Va a recibir una notificación por una infracción.

▬▬ II. ACTION SCENE COGNATES

infraction	la infracción
persons	las personas

license	la licencia
telephone	el teléfono
dark	oscuro
vehicle	el vehículo
velocity	la velocidad
ambulance	la ambulancia

III. ACTION SCENE VOCABULARY

seat belt	el cinturón de seguridad
to hurt	doler
Do you hurt?	¿Le duele?
hurt	lastimado (a)
tow truck	la grúa
to open	abrir
head	la cabeza
Is there?/Are there?	¿Hay . . . ?
broken	descompuesta/o
traffic light	el semáforo

Interrogatives

Where?	¿Dónde?
From where?	¿De dónde?
Who?	¿Quién?
What?	¿Qué?
At what time?	¿A qué hora?
On what street?	¿En qué calle?
To where?	¿Adónde?
On where?	¿En dónde?
Which, what?	¿Cuál?

Commands

Give me . . .	Deme . . .
Calm down.	Cálmese.
Do not move.	No se mueva.

IV. EXPANDED VOCABULARY

bandage	la venda
rapid	rápido
collision/accident	el choque
he/she was	fue
run over	atropellado
witness	el testigo
evidence	la prueba
indicted	procesado
fine	la multa
crime	el delito
seat belt	el cinturón de seguridad
lights on	la luces encendidas/las luces puestas
turn	doblar
to the right/on the right	a la derecha
to the left/on the left	a la izquierda
glasses	los lentes
What happened?	¿Qué ocurrió?, ¿Qué pasó?
At what time?	¿A qué hora?
Was it dark?	¿Estaba oscuro?
Was it raining?	¿Llovía?/¿Estaba lloviendo?
Was it snowing?	¿Nevaba?/¿Estaba nevando?
Was there	¿Había
water on the street?	agua en la calle?
ice on the street?	hielo en la calle?

V. ACTION SCENE STRUCTURAL EXERCISES

1. (I am) _____ policía.

2. ¿Quién es (the driver) _____?

3. ¿Está (injured) _____?

4. ¿(Where) _____ le duele?

5. Calm down _____.

VI. ACTION SCENE STRUCTURAL EXERCISE

1. ¿Hay alguien más en el vehículo?
2. ¿Dónde le duele?
3. ¿Está lastimado?
4. ¿A qué velocidad iba?
5. ¿Había un problema mecánico?
6. ¿Dónde trabaja?
7. ¿A qué hora?

VII. ACTION SCENARIOS

1. You arrive at the scene of a traffic accident. There is a single driver who is injured.
   a. Identify yourself.
   b. Is anyone else in the vehicle?
   c. Where do you hurt?
   d. Do you hurt when you move?
   e. Calm down.
   f. The ambulance is on the way.
   g. Don't move.

2. You arrive at the scene of a traffic accident where the victims are uninjured.
   a. Identify yourself.
   b. Move the vehicle over there.
   c. Is anyone injured?
   d. Show me
      1. your driver's license.
      2. your insurance papers.
      3. your car registration papers.

3. Continue with the accident investigation.
   a. Who was driving the vehicle?
   b. Where did the accident occur?
   c. At what time did the accident occur?
   d. What street were you on?

4. Decide what to do with the vehicles.
   a. Is it possible to drive the vehicle?
   b. The tow truck is coming.
   c. You are going to receive a notification of an infraction.

CHAPTER 15   TRAFFIC ACCIDENT: VIDEO SCRIPT

I. ACTION SCENE: INJURED VICTIMS

I am the police.	Soy policía.
Is anyone else in the vehicle?	¿Hay alguien más en el vehículo?
No.	*No.*
Where do you hurt?	¿Dónde le duele?
Here and here.	*Aquí y aquí.*
Do you hurt when you move?	¿Le duele cuando se mueve?
Yes.	*Sí.*
I am going to apply this (a bandage).	Voy a ponerle esto (una venda).
Do not move.	No se mueva.
¡Ay!	*¡Ay!*
Tell me if it hurts you.	Dígame si le duele.
Calm down.	Cálmese.
The ambulance is on the way.	Ya viene la ambulancia.

Action Scene: Uninjured Victims

Are you the driver of the car?	¿Es usted el conductor del vehículo?
Yes.	*Sí.*
Is anyone injured?	¿Está lastimado?
No.	*No.*
Is anyone else in your vehicle?	¿Hay alguien más en el vehículo?
No.	*No.*

Investigation

Show me	Enséñeme
your driver's license.	su licencia de manejar.
your insurance papers.	sus papeles del seguro.
car registration papers.	sus papeles del registro.
Is the information correct on your license?	¿Es correcta la información en su licencia?
Yes.	*Sí.*
Your address?	¿Su dirección?
85 North Admiral St.	*Ochenta y cinco norte calle Admiral.*

Your telephone number?

    8-80-36-18

Where do you work?

    At the Acapulco Hotel.

Who was driving the vehicle?

    I was.

At what time did the accident occur?

    About 15 minutes ago.

Was it raining?

    No.

What street were you on?

    At 5th and Louis.

Where were you going?

    To my house.

Were you trying to turn
to the right?

    Yes.

Did you signal the turn?

    Yes.

Where did the other vehicle
come from?

    It came from the front.

How fast were you going?

    15 miles per hour.

Was the traffic light

    red?

    yellow?

    green?

    Green.

Did you stop?

    Yes.

Did the other vehicle stop?

    No.

Was there a mechanical problem?

    No.

Were you wearing your seat belt?

    Yes.

¿Su teléfono?

    Ocho, ochenta, treinta y seis, diez y ocho.

¿Dónde trabaja?

    En el Hotel Acapulco.

¿Quién estaba manejando el vehículo?

    Yo.

¿A qué hora ocurrió el accidente?

    Hace quince minutos.

¿Llovía?

    No.

¿En qué calle estaba?

    En la Cinco y Louis.

¿Adónde iba?

    Para mi casa.

¿Estaba tratando de doblar
a la derecha?

    Sí.

¿Hizo alguna señal?

    Sí.

¿De dónde venía el otro
vehículo?

    Venía de frente.

¿A qué velocidad iba?

    Quince millas por hora.

¿El semáforo estaba

    rojo?

    amarillo?

    verde?

    Verde.

¿Se detuvo?

    Sí.

¿Se detuvo el otro vehículo?

    No.

¿Había un problema mecánico en su
vehículo?

    No.

¿Se puso el cinturón de seguridad?

    Sí.

Moving The Vehicle

Is it possible to drive the vehicle?	¿Es posible manejar su vehículo?
No.	*No.*
A tow truck is coming.	Ya viene la grúa.
Do not move.	No se mueva.
You are receiving a (citation/ warning) notification for an infraction.	Va a recibir una notificación por una infracción.

16

Consent Search

I. ACTION SCENE: SUSPECT

I am the police.	Soy policía.
Take your hands out of your pockets.	Saque las manos de los bolsillos.
Where are you going?	¿A dónde va?
Where are you coming from?	¿De dónde viene usted?
How long have you been travelling?	¿Desde cuándo está viajando?
Whose vehicle is this?	¿De quién es el vehículo?
How often do you put gasoline in it (the vehicle)?	¿Cada cuándo le pone gasolina?
Open the trunk.	Abra la cajuela.
Does your spare tire have air?	¿Tiene aire su llanta de refacción?
Do you have drugs in the vehicle?	¿Tiene drogas en el vehículo?
Do you have weapons in the vehicle?	¿Tiene armas en el vehículo?
Stand there.	Párese allá.

II. ACTION SCENE COGNATES

gasoline	la gasolina
drugs	las drogas
arms	las armas

III. ACTION SCENE VOCABULARY

trunk	la cajuela
spare tire	la llanta de refacción

Commands

Get out of the car.	Salga del vehículo.

IV. EXPANDED VOCABULARY

highway	la carretera
door	la puerta
glove compartment	la guantera
street	la calle
I am going to search you.	Lo voy a revisar.
You are under arrest.	Está arrestado.

V. ACTION SCENE STRUCTURAL EXERCISE

1. ¿Desde cuándo (have you been traveling) _____?
2. Where are you coming from? ¿_____?
3. (How long) ¿_____?
4. (Get out of the car) _____.
5. (Whose) ¿_____ este vehículo?
6. (Open the trunk) _____.
7. ¿Tiene aire (your spare tire) _____?
8. (Do you have drugs) ¿_____ en el vehículo?

VI. ACTION SCENE SCENARIOS

1. You have stopped a vehicle for a traffic violation.

    a. Identify yourself.

    b. Where are you going?

    c. Are you going to stay with him/her?

    d. What is his address?

    e. Where are you coming from?

    f. Take your hands out of your pockets.

2. You are continuing with Scenario 1.

    a. Whose vehicle is this?

    b. How often do you put gasoline in the car?

    c. Get out of the vehicle.

    d. Open the trunk.

    e. Stand here.

3. You are continuing with Scenario 1.

    a. Does your spare tire have air?

    b. Do you have drugs in the vehicle?

    c. Do you have weapons in the vehicle?

    d. Extend your arms.

    e. You are under arrest.

CHAPTER 16 CONSENT SEARCH: VIDEO SCRIPT

I. ACTION SCENE: SUSPECT

I am the police.	Soy policía.
Take your hands out of your pockets.	Saque las manos de los bolsillos.
Where are you going?	¿A dónde va?
To Laredo, Texas to visit a friend.	*A Laredo, Texas a visitar a un amigo.*
Will you stay with him?	¿Va a quedarse con él?
Yes.	*Sí.*
What is his address?	¿Cuál es la dirección de él?
I do not remember.	*No recuerdo.*
Where are you coming from?	¿De dónde viene usted?
From Tulsa, Oklahoma.	*De Tulsa, Oklahoma.*
How long have you been travelling?	¿Desde cuándo está viajando?
About 2 hours.	*Hace dos horas.*
Whose vehicle is this?	¿De quién es el vehículo?
It is mine.	*Es mío.*
How often do you put gasoline in it (the vehicle)?	¿Cada cuándo le pone gasolina?
Every week.	*Cada ocho días.*
Open the trunk.	Abra la cajuela.

Does your spare tire have air?   ¿Tiene aire su llanta de refacción?
  Yes.   *Sí.*
Do you have drugs in the vehicle?   ¿Tiene drogas en el vehículo?
  No.   *No.*
Do you have weapons in the vehicle?   ¿Tiene armas en el vehículo?
  No.   *No.*
Stand there.   Párese allá.

PART IV

TACTICAL OPERATIONS

Warrant Execution

I. ACTION SCENE: COMMANDS

I am the police.	Soy policía.
I have a search warrant!	¡Tengo una orden de revisión!*
Get on the ground.	Todos al piso.
On your knees.	De rodillas.
Hands over your head.	Manos sobre la cabeza.
Do not move.	No se mueva.
Is there anyone else in the house?	¿Hay alguien más en la casa?
Do you have any weapons.	¿Tiene armas?
I am going to handcuff you.	Lo voy a esposar.

*Also "registro."

II. ACTION SCENE COGNATES

arms	las armas
search	la revisión

III. ACTION SCENE VOCABULARY

floor	el piso
search warrant	la orden de revisión

on your knees	de rodillas
head	la cabeza
hands	las manos
someone	alguien
to handcuff	esposar
handcuffs	las esposas

IV. EXPANDED VOCABULARY

Get into the vehicle!	¡Suba al vehículo!
Move over here.	Muévase para acá.
Outside!	¡Fuera!
Come out.	Salga.
Stop!	¡Alto!
Hands up.	Manos arriba.
Put your hands behind your back.	Manos atrás.
Follow me.	Sígame.
Get up.	Levántese.
Take out your hands slowly.	Saque las manos despacio.
Drop the pistol.	Suelte la pistola.
Drop it!	¡Suéltelo!/¡Suéltela!
One step forward,	Un paso al frente.
One step back.	Un paso atrás,
Look at the wall.	Mire la pared.
Put your hands on the car.	Ponga las manos sobre el vehículo.
Silence!	¡Silencio!
Calm down.	Cálmese.
Cross your feet.	Cruce los pies.
Arms out.	Brazos afuera.
Palms up.	Palmas arriba.
Do you understand?	¿Entiende?
Do you understand your rights?	¿Entiende sus derechos?
warrant for arrest	la orden de arrestar

V. ACTION SCENE STRUCTURAL EXERCISE

1. Tengo (a search warrant.) _____.

2. (Hands above your head.) _____.

3. (Kneel down.) _____.

4. ¿Tiene (weapons) _____?

5. (Is there) ¿_____ alguien más en la casa?

6. Lo voy a _____ (handcuff.)

VI. ACTION SCENARIOS

1. On patrol, you have a search warrant for a young woman who is inside of a mobile home.

    a. Identify yourself.

    b. I have a search warrant.

    c. Hands over your head.

    d. Do not move.

    e. Stop.

2. You are finishing the commands for Scenario 1.

    a. Kneel down.

    b. Do you have weapons?

    c. Is there someone else in the house?

    d. I am going to handcuff you.

    e. Get into the vehicle.

CHAPTER 17 WARRANT EXECUTION: VIDEO SCRIPT

I. ACTION SCENE: COMMANDS

I am the police.	Soy policía.
I have a search warrant!	¡Tengo una orden de revisión!*
Get on the ground.	Todos al piso.
On your knees.	De rodillas.
Hands over your head.	Manos sobre la cabeza.
Do not move.	No se mueva.

———
*Also "registro."

Is there anyone else in the house?	¿Hay alguien más en la casa?
No.	*No.*
Do you have any weapons?	¿Tiene armas?
No.	*No.*
I am going to handcuff you.	Lo voy a esposar.

Dangerous Command by Suspects

Disarm him/her.	Desármelo/la.
Jump him/her.	Sáltelo/la.
Shoot him/her.	Disparele.
Take his/her gun.	Quítele la pistola.
Run.	Córrale.

C H A P T E R

18

High Risk (Felony) Vehicle Stop

I. ACTION SCENE: DRIVER/PASSENGER

I am the police.	Soy policía.
You are under arrest.	Está arrestado.
Do not turn around.	No voltee.
Do not move.	No se mueva.
Put your hands over your head.	Ponga las manos sobre su cabeza.

To a Driver

With your left hand turn off the motor.	Con la mano izquierda apague el motor.

DO IT NOW!	¡Hágalo ahora!
Repeat after each command	

With your left hand roll down your window.	Con la mano izquierda abra la ventana.
With your left hand, throw the keys towards the sound of my voice.	Con la mano izquierda tire las llaves hacia el sonido de mi voz.
Open the door.	¡Abra la puerta!
Step out of the vehicle.	Salga del vehículo.

Visual Search and Movement Commands to Driver/Passenger

Keep your hands up high.	Mantenga sus manos arriba.
Take two steps away from the vehicle to your left/right.	Aléjese dos pasos del vehículo hacia su izquierda/derecha.
With your left hand lift the back of your shirt.	Con la mano izquierda levante la parte de atrás de su camisa.
Turn around slowly.	Voltéese despacio.
Stop.	Alto.
Keep on (turning).	Siga.
Walk backward toward my voice.	Camine para atrás hacia el sonido de mi voz.
Kneel down.	De rodillas.

Handcuff and Interrogate

Kneel down.	De rodillas.
Keep your hands up.	Mantenga sus manos arriba.
Put your hands over your head.	Ponga sus manos sobre la cabeza.
Interlock your fingers.	Cruce sus dedos de las manos.
I am going to handcuff you.	Lo voy a esposar.
Put your right hand down.	Baje su mano derecha.
Put your left hand down.	Baje su mano izquierda.
Do you hand any weapons?	¿Tiene armas?
How many passengers are there?	¿Cuántos pasajeros hay?
Get up.	Levántese.

II. ACTION SCENE COGNATES

You are under arrest.	Está arrestado.
voice	la voz
vehicle	el vehículo
arms	las armas
passengers	los pasajeros

III. ACTION SCENE VOCABULARY

right hand	la mano derecha
left hand	la mano izquierda
sound	el sonido

Interrogatives

how many	¿Cuántos?

Commands

Do not turn around.	No voltee.
Turn around slowly.	Voltéese despacio.
Do not move.	No se mueva.
Put your hands	Ponga las manos
on your head.	en su cabeza.
behind your head.	atrás de su cabeza.
over your head.	sobre su cabeza.
Turn off the motor.	Apague el motor.
Roll down your window.	Baje su ventana.
Throw the keys.	Tire las llaves.
Open the door.	Abra la puerta.
Get out of the vehicle.	Salga del vehículo.
Hands up.	Manos arriba.
Keep your hands up.	Mantenga sus manos arriba.
Take two steps away from the vehicle.	Aléjese dos pasos del vehículo.
Stop.	Alto.
Walk backward.	Camine para atrás.
On your knees.	De rodillas.
Get on the ground./Get on the floor.	Al suelo./Al piso.
Face down.	Boca abajo.
Get up.	Levántese.
Get in the vehicle.	Suba al vehículo.
Do it now.	Hágalo ahora.
Right now.	Ahora mismo.

IV. EXPANDED VOCABULARY

Face down.	Boca abajo.
Get in the back of the vehicle.	Suba a la parte de atrás del vehículo.
I am going to handcuff you.	Lo voy a esposar.
Move to the left/right side of the car.	Muévase a la parte izquierda/derecha del coche.

Stop or I'll shoot.	Alto o disparo.
Do not run.	No corra.
Your conduct is illegal.	Su conducta es ilegal.
Throw your weapon on the ground.	Tire el arma al suelo.
Sit down.	Siéntese.
Be quiet.	Silencio.
Move.	Muévase.

V. ACTION SCENE STRUCTURAL EXERCISE

1. (You are under arrest) _____.
2. (Do not turn around) _____.
3. (Do not move) _____.
4. Ponga sus manos (behind your head) _____.
5. (Turn off the motor) _____.
6. (Open the door) _____.
7. (Get out of the car) _____.
8. (Turn around) _____.

VI. ACTION SCENARIOS

1. You are a police officer on motorized patrol. You see a stolen vehicle and signal it to stop. Using the public address system of your patrol car, speak to the single passenger.

   a. Identify yourself.

   b. You are under arrest.

   c. Stop.

   d. Get out of the car.

   e. Do not turn around.

   f. Do not move.

2. You are continuing with Scenario 1.

   a. With your left hand, roll down the window.

   b. With your left hand, throw the keys toward the sound of my voice.

   c. Open the door.

   d. Step out of the vehicle.

3. You are continuing with Scenario 1.

   a. Keep you hands up.

   b. Keep your hands up high.

   c. Take two steps away from the vehicle to your left.

   d. Turn around slowly.

   e. Kneel down.

4. You are continuing with Scenario 1.

   a. Place your hands on the back of your head.

   b. Interlock your fingers.

   c. Put your left hand down.

   d. Do you have any weapons?

   e. I am going to handcuff you.

5. You are continuing with Scenario 1.

   a. Keep your hands up.

   b. Walk backward.

   c. On your knees.

   d. Get up.

   e. Get in the vehicle.

CHAPTER 18   HIGH RISK (FELONY) VEHICLE STOP: VIDEO SCRIPT

I. ACTION SCENE: DRIVER/PASSENGER

I am the police.	Soy policía.
You are under arrest.	Está arrestado.
Do not turn around.	No voltee.
Do not move.	No se mueva.
Put your hands over your head.	Ponga las manos sobre su cabeza.

To a Driver

With your left hand turn off the ignition.   Con la mano izquierda apague el motor.

DO IT NOW!	¡Hágalo ahora!
Repeat after each command	

With your left hand roll down your window.

Con la mano izquierda abra la ventana.

With your left hand, throw the keys towards the sound of my voice.

Con la mano izquierda, tire las llaves hacia el sonido de mi voz.

Open the door.

¡Abra la puerta!

Step out of the vehicle.

Salga del vehículo.

Visual Search and Movement Commands to Driver/Passenger

Keep your hands up high.

Mantenga sus manos arriba.

Take two steps away from the vehicle to your left/right.

Aléjese dos pasos del vehículo hacia su izquierda/derecha.

With your left hand lift the back of your shirt.

Con la mano izquierda levante la parte de atrás de su camisa.

Turn around slowly.

Voltéese despacio.

Stop.

Alto.

Keep on (turning).

Siga.

Walk backward toward my voice.

Camine para atrás hacia mi voz.

Kneel down.

De rodillas.

Handcuff and Interrogate

Kneel down.

De rodillas.

Keep your hands up.

Mantenga sus manos arriba.

Put your hands over your head.

Ponga sus manos sobre la cabeza.

Interlock your fingers.

Cruce sus dedos de las manos.

I am going to handcuff you.

Lo voy a esposar.

Put your left hand down.

Baje su mano derecha.

Put your right hand down.

Baje su mano izquierda.

Do you have any weapons?

¿Tiene armas?

No.

No.

How many passengers are there?

¿Cuántos pasajeros hay?

None.

Ninguno.

Get up.

Levántese.

CHAPTER

19

Suspicious Person: Arrest/No Arrrest

▨ **I. ACTION SCENE: SUSPECT ARREST**

Come here.	Venga aquí.
What is going on?	¿Qué pasa?
Take your hands out of your pockets.	Saque las manos de sus bolsillos.
Stay here.	Quédese aquí.
Do not move.	No se mueva.
Give me your identification.	Déme su identificación.

Personal Data Questions

What is your name?	¿Cómo se llama?
Your address?	¿Su dirección?
Daytime telephone number?	¿Su teléfono durante el día?
Nighttime telephone number?	¿Su teléfono durante la noche?
Age?	¿Su edad?
Date of birth?	¿Su fecha de nacimiento?
Where do you work?	¿Dónde trabaja?

Investigation

Where are you going?	¿Adónde va?
Do you live here?	¿Vive aquí?
Are you waiting for a friend?	¿Está esperando a un amigo?
Since when?	¿Desde cuándo?
What is your friend's name?	¿Cómo se llama su amigo?
Do you have any weapons?	¿Tiene usted armas?
I am going to search you.	Lo voy a revisar. *
Turn around.	Voltéese.

———

*Legal usage "to search" is "registrar." "Revisar" is used widely.

Arrest

Hands over your head.	Manos sobre la cabeza.
Separate your legs.	Separe las piernas.
This weapon is illegal.	Esta arma es ilegal.
I am going to handcuff you.	Lo voy a esposar.
You are under arrest.	Está arrestado.

No Arrest

Leave.	Váyase.
Leave here.	Salga de aquí.

II. ACTION SCENE COGNATES

identification	la identificación
arms, weapons	las armas
illegal	ilegal
to arrest	arrestar
You are under arrest.	Está usted arrestado.

Interrogatives

What?	¿Qué?
What is your name?	¿Cómo se llama?
Who?	¿Quién?
How many?	¿Cuántos?

Where are you going?	¿Adónde va?
When?	¿Cuándo?
Since when?	¿Desde cuándo?
How old are you?	¿Cuántos años tiene?

Commands

Stay here.	Quédese aquí.
Do not move.	No se mueva.
Show me.	Enséñeme.
Leave from here.	Salga de aquí.

III. ACTION SCENE VOCABULARY

Are you waiting for a friend?	¿Está esperando a un amigo?
Do you have weapons?	¿Tiene armas?
to work	trabajar
Do you work here?	¿Trabaja aquí?
to live	vivir
Do you live here?	¿Vive aquí?
I am going to search you.	Lo voy a registrar*.

————

*Also "revisar," "escular" (non-standard).

IV. EXPANDED VOCABULARY

Nothing is going on.	No pasa nada.
I do not have weapons.	No tengo armas.
I do not know.	No sé.
I have no idea.	No tengo idea.
Who knows?	¿Quién sabe?

V. ACTION SCENE STRUCTURAL EXERCISE

1. (Come here) _____ _____.
2. (What is going on?) ¿_____?
3. (Stay here) _____.
4. (Do not move) _____.

5. Déme (your identification) _____.

6. (Do you work) ¿_____ aquí?

7. (Where are you going) ¿ _____?

8. ¿Tiene (weapons) _____?

9. Voy a (search you) _____.

10. (You are under arrest) _____.

VI. ACTION SCENE QUESTIONS

1. (What is going on?) ¿_____?

2. (Do you live) ¿ _____ aquí?

3. (Do you work) ¿_____ aquí?

4. (Leave) _____.

VII. ACTION SCENARIO

1. You have stopped a suspect on the street.

   a. Identify yourself.

   b. Come here.

   c. Do not move.

   d. Show me your identification.

   e. What is going on?

2. You are continuing with questioning a suspect in Scenario 1.

   a. Ask Personal Data Questions.

   b. Do you work here?

   c. How old are you?

   d. Do you live here?

3. You are continuing with the questions for Scenario 3.

   a. What is your friend's name?

   b. When will he/she return?

   c. Do you have weapons?

   d. I am gong to search you.

   e. This weapon is illegal.

   If an arrest is to be made:

   f. You are under arrest.

   If no arrest is to be made:

   g. Leave here.

CHAPTER 19 SUSPICIOUS PERSON: ARREST/NO ARRREST: VIDEO SCRIPT

I. ACTION SCENE: SUSPECT ARREST

Come here.	Venga aquí.
What is going on?	¿Qué pasa?
Nothing.	*Nada.*
Take your hands out of your pockets.	Saque las manos de sus bolsillos.
Stay here.	Quédese aquí.
Do not move.	No se mueva.
Give me your identification.	Déme su identificación.
No.	*No.*

Personal Data Questions (not in video)

What is your name?	¿Cómo se llama?
Your address?	¿Su dirección?
Daytime telephone number?	¿Su teléfono durante el día?
Nighttime telephone number?	¿Su teléfono durante la noche?
Age?	¿Su edad?
Date of birth?	¿Su fecha de nacimiento?
Where do you work?	¿Dónde trabaja?

Investigation

Where are you going?	¿Adónde va?
Over there.	*Allá.*
Do you live here?	¿Vive aquí?
No.	*No.*
Are you waiting for a friend?	¿Está esperando a un amigo?
Yes.	*Sí.*
Since when?	¿Desde cuándo?
I do not know.	*No sé.*
What is your friend's name?	¿Cómo se llama su amigo?
Pablo.	*Pablo.*

Do you have any weapons?	¿Tiene usted armas?
No.	*No.*
I am going to search you.	Lo voy a revisar. *
Turn around.	Voltéese.

———

*Legal usage "to search" is "registrar." "Revisar" is used widely.

If an Arrest is to Be Made

Hands over your head.	Manos sobre la cabeza.
Separate your legs.	Separe las piernas.
This weapon is illegal.	Esta arma es ilegal.
I am going to handcuff you.	Lo voy a esposar.
You are under arrest.	Está arrestado.

PART V

PENAL INSTITUTIONS

Booking Procedures

I. ACTION SCENE

Take everything out of your pockets.	Saque todo de sus bolsillos.
Place the things here.	Ponga todo aquí.
Sit down.	Siéntese.
Why have you been arrested?	¿Por qué está arrestada?

Personal Data Questions

What is your name?	¿Cómo se llama?
Your address?	¿Su dirección?
Daytime telephone number?	¿Su teléfono durante el día?
Nighttime telephone number?	¿Su teléfono durante la noche?
Date of birth?	¿Su fecha de nacimiento?
Age?	¿Su edad?
Where were you born?	¿Dónde nació?
Where do you work?	¿Dónde trabaja?

Stand here, please.	Párese aquí, por favor.
Are you a citizen of this country?	¿Es usted ciudadana /o de este país?
What is your social security number?	¿Cuál es el número de su seguro social?
How tall are you?	¿Cuánto mide?
How much do you weigh?	¿Cuánto pesa?

Who do we contact in case of an emergency?	En caso de emergencia, ¿a quién podemos llamar?
What is that person's address?	¿Cuál es la dirección de esa persona?
What is that person's telephone number?	¿Cuál es el número de teléfono de esa persona?
Have you ever been arrested before?	¿La /lo han arrestado antes?
Where?	¿Dónde?
Why?	¿Por qué?
Have you been in this jail before?	¿Ha estado en esta cárcel antes?
This is a list of the property we have in custody.	Esta es una lista de las propiedades que tenemos bajo custodia.
If it is correct, sign here.	Si es correcta, firme aquí.
Do you want to call someone?	¿Quiere llamar a alguien?
Here is the telephone.	Aquí está el teléfono.

II. ACTION SCENE COGNATES

telephone	teléfono
social security	el seguro social
emergency	la emergencia
correct	correcto
to arrest	arrestar
he was arrested	fue arrestado
list	la lista
property	la propiedad

Interrogatives

Where?	¿Dónde?
How much?	¿Cuánto?
What is ____ ?	¿Cuál es ___ ?
Why?	¿Por qué?
When?	¿Cuándo?

III. ACTION SCENE VOCABULARY

pockets	los bolsillos
to measure (height)	medir

How tall are you?	¿Cuánto mide?
to be born	nacer
Where were you born?	¿Dónde nació?
to weigh	pesar
How much do you weigh?	¿Cuánto pesa?
to call	llamar
Do you want to call anyone?	¿Quiere llamar a alguien?
How old are you?	¿Cuántos años tiene?

Commands

stand here	párese
take out	saque
take out everything	saque todo
Sign here.	Firme aquí.
Put it here.	Póngalo/la aquí.
Sit down.	Siéntese.
Wait.	Espere.

IV. EXPANDED VOCABULARY

drug possession	la posesión de drogas
drug dealing	la venta de drogas
car theft	el robo de coches
homocide	el homicidio
to kill someone	matar a alguien
assault	el asalto
drunk driving	manejar borracho
speeding	el exceso de velocidad
spousal abuse	abusar de la esposa
robbery, theft	robo
child abuse	el abuso de los niños
public drunkeness	emborarracharse en público
to need	necesitar
to post bond	depositar una fianza
speak with an attorney	hablar con un abogado
a nickname	un apodo

V. ACTION SCENE STRUCTURAL EXERCISE

1. (Stand here) _____.

2. Saque todo de (your pockets) _____.

3. (What is your name) ¿_____?

4. ¿Tiene (a nickname) _____ ?

5. ¿Dónde (were you born) _____?

6. ¿Cuál es (your Social Security number) _____?

7. ¿Cuál es (your work telephone number) _____?

8. En caso de emergencia, ¿a quién debemos (call) _____?

9. (Have you been arrested) ¿_____ antes?

10. ¿Ha estado (in this jail) _____ antes?

VI. ACTION SCENE QUESTIONS

1. ¿Dónde nació?

2. ¿Cuál es su número de teléfono?

3. ¿Cuál es su número del seguro social?

4. ¿Dónde trabaja?

5. ¿Cuál es la dirección de su trabajo?

6. ¿En caso de emergencia, a quién debemos llamar?

7. ¿Lo han arrestado antes?

8. ¿Ha estado en esta cárcel antes?

9. ¿Quiere llamar a alguien?

VII. ACTION SCENARIOS

1. You are the officer in charge of booking a suspect.

    a. Stand here.

    b. Take everything out of your pockets.

    c. Place the things here.

    d. Sit down.

2. Continue with Scenario 1.

    a. Ask Personal Information Questions.

    b. Where were you born?

3. Continue with the booking process in Scenario 1.

    a. Where do you work?

    b. When do you work?

    c. What is your work address?

    d. What is your social security number?

    e. How tall are you?

    f. How much do you weigh?

4. You are booking another suspect.

    a. Have you been arrested before?

        1. Why?

        2. When?

    b. Have you been in this jail before?

        1. Why?

        2. When?

    c. Do you want to call someone?

        1. Here is the telephone.

CHAPTER 20   BOOKING PROCEDURES: VIDEO SCRIPT

I. ACTION SCENE

Take everything out of your pockets.	Saque todo de sus bolsillos.
Place the things here.	Ponga todo aquí.
(19 cents, keys, a pair of earrings, and a package of cigarettes.)	*(Diez y nueve centavos, llaves, un par de aretes y un paquete de cigarros.)*
Sit down.	Siéntese.
Why have you been arrested?	¿Por qué está arrestada?
For prostitution.	*Por prostitución.*

Personal Data Questions

What is your name?	¿Cómo se llama?
Sandra Lopez.	*Sandra López.*
Your address?	¿Su dirección?
469 5th Street	*Cuatrocientos sesenta y nueve Calle Cinco*

Daytime telephone number?
> *918-5-8-2-4-1-2-1*

¿Su teléfono durante el día?
> *Novecientos diez y ocho cinco, ocho, dos, cuatro, uno, dos, uno.*

Nighttime telephone number?
> *It is the same.*

¿Su teléfono durante la noche?
> *Es el mismo.*

Date of birth?
> *May 2, 1963.*

¿Su fecha de nacimiento?
> *Dos de mayo de mil novecientos sesenta y tres*

Age?
> *36*

¿Su edad?
> *Treinta y seis años.*

Where were you born?
> *In Nuevo Leon.*

¿Dónde nació?
> *En Nuevo León.*

Where do you work?
> *At the Roma Hotel.*

¿Dónde trabaja?
> *En el Hotel "Roma"*

Stand here, please.

Párese aquí, por favor.

Are you a citizen of this country?
> *Yes.*

¿Es usted ciudadana de este país?
> *Sí*

What is your social security number?

> *4-4-4-6-5-3-4-0-1*

¿Cuál es el número de su seguro social?

> *Cuatro, cuatro, cuatro, seis cinco, tres, cuatro, cero, uno.*

How tall are you?
> *5' 4"*

¿Cuánto mide?
> *Cinco pies cuatro pulgadas.*

How much do you weigh?
> *140 pounds.*

¿Cuánto pesa?
> *Ciento cuarenta libras.*

Who do we contact in case of an emergency?
> *Mi mother, Blanca Lopez.*

En caso de emergencia, ¿a quién podemos llamar?
> *A mi madre, Blanca López.*

What is that person's address?
> *501 11th Street.*

¿Cuál es la dirección de esa persona?
> *Quinientos uno Calle Once.*

What is that person's telephone number?
> *269-24-0-5*

¿Cuál es el número de teléfono de esa persona?
> *Doscientos sesenta y nueve, veinte y cuatro, cero, cinco.*

Have you ever been arrested before?
> *Yes.*

¿Lo/la han arrestado antes?
> *Sí.*

Where?
> *In Arizona.*

¿Dónde?
> *En Arizona.*

Why?	¿Por qué?
Because I was drunk.	*Porque estaba borracha.*
Have you been in this jail before?	¿Ha estado en esta cárcel antes?
No.	*No.*
This is a list of the property we have in custody.	Esta es una lista de las propiedades que tenemos bajo custodia.
If it is correct, sign here.	Si es correcta, firme aquí.
Do you want to call someone?	¿Quiere llamar a alguien?
Yes.	*Sí.*
Here is the telephone.	Aquí está el teléfono.

Cultural note: Last Names

In Spanish-speaking countries, a person will often carry both his/her father's family name and mother's family name.

For example: *Guillermo López Mateos*

López = father's family name
Mateos = mother's family name

When *María Romero Díaz* marries Guillermo López Mateos, she becomes *María Romero de López*. Therefore, she will keep her father's last name and add her husband's father's family name.

Cultural note: Nicknames

Nicknames are common in Spanish speaking countries. For example, they may describe a physical characteristic such as "El chaparro Híjar" (Shorty Híjar), "el roto", "el pelón", "la changa", "el oso", "el cholo", "la marrana", "el negro", "el ratón", "la gringa", "le chata", "la morena", "la güera".

Spanish slang/nickname	Possible nickname translation
"el roto"	the broken, raggedy one
"el pelón"	the bald one
"el oso"	the bear
"la marrana"	the swine/hog/pig
"el ratón"	the rat
"el gringo"	the foreigner (esp. North American)
"el chato"	the flat nose
"la morena"	the brunette/the dark one/the dark-skinned one
"la güera"	the blonde, fair skinned

C H A P T E R

21

Correctional Officer Commands

I. ACTION SCENES

Stay in line.	Quédese en la línea.
Be quiet.	Silencio.
Remain standing.	Quédese parado.
Where do you live?	¿Dónde vive?
Show me your identification.	Déme su identificación.
Where is your cellmate?	¿Dónde está su compañero?
Are you in a gang?	¿Está en una pandilla?/una ganga?/ un grupo?
I am going to search you.	Lo voy a revisar.
Put your hands out to your sides.	Extienda los brazos a los lados.
Turn around.	Voltéese.
What is in your pocket?	¿Qué hay en sus bolsillos?
Empty your pockets.	Vacíe sus bolsillos.
Sit down.	Siéntese.
Take off your shoes.	Quítese los zapatos.
Get up.	Levántese.
You have a visitor.	Tiene una visita.
I am going to write a report.	Voy a escribir un reporte.

II. ACTION SCENE COGNATES

identification	la identificación

Commands

Silence	Silencio
Move	Muévase
Sit down	Siéntese
Get up	Levántese
Stay	Quédese
Go	Váyase
Empty	Vacíe

III. ACTION SCENE VOCABULARY

the line	la línea
house (cell)	la casa
I am going to search you.	Lo voy a revisar.
pockets	los bolsillos

Interrogatives

Where	¿Dónde?
What is there?	¿Qué hay?
What happened?	¿Qué pasó?

IV. EXPANDED VOCABULARY

Leave here.	Salga de aquí.
Give me your hand.	Déme la mano.
Do not look at me.	No me mire.
The lawyer is coming.	Viene el abogado.

Medical

Do you need a doctor?	¿Necesita un doctor?

Commands

Go to the recreation area.	Váyase al área de recreo.
Go to your cell (house).	Váyase a su celda (casa).
Go eat.	Váyase a comer.

V. ACTION SCENE STRUCTURAL EXERCISE

1. (Stay in line) _____.
2. (Go to your cell) _____.
3. Enséñeme (your identification) _____.
4. (I am going to search you). _____.

VI. ACTION SCENARIOS

1. You are a correctional officer in a maximum-security facility.

Issue the Following Commands/Questions

   a. Stay in line.
   b. Stop.
   c. Where do you live?
   d. Show me your identification.
   e. Slowly.
   f. Be quiet.

2. You are continuing with Scenario 1.
   a. Where is your cellmate?
   b. Are you in a gang?
   c. Remain standing.
   d. I am going to search you.
   e. Put your hands out to the sides.
   f. Turn around.

3. You are continuing with Scenario 1.
   a. Empty your pockets.
   b. Sit down.
   c. Take off your shoes.
   d. Get up.
   e. Move.
   f. I am going to write a report.

4. You are an officer continuing with Scenario 1.

    a. Do you need a doctor?

    b. Go to the recreational area.

    c. Go to your cell.

    d. Go to eat.

    e. You have a visitor.

CHAPTER 21   CORRECTIONAL OFFICER COMMANDS: VIDEO SCRIPT

I. ACTION SCENES

Stay in line.	Quédese en la línea.
Be quiet.	Silencio.
Remain standing.	Quédese parado.
Where do you live?	¿Dónde vive?
Show me your identification.	Déme su identificación.
Where is your cellmate?	¿Dónde está su compañero?
Are you in a gang?	¿Está en... una pandilla? una ganga? un grupo?
I am going to search you.	Lo voy a revisar.
Put your hands out to your sides.	Extienda los brazos a los lados.
Turn around.	Voltéese.
What is in your pockets?	¿Qué hay en sus bolsillos?
Empty your pockets.	Vacíe sus bolsillos.
Sit down.	Siéntese.
Take off your shoes.	Quítese los zapatos.
Get up.	Levántese.
You have a visitor.	Tiene una visita.
I am going to write a report.	Voy a escribir un reporte.

PART VI

TELECOMMUNICATIONS

Emergency Telecommunicator

I. ACTION SCENE: TELECOMMUNICATION OPERATOR

911. What is your emergency?	911. ¿Cuál es su emergencia?
Your name?	¿Su nombre?
Your address?	¿Su dirección?
Your telephone number?	¿Su teléfono?
Are you with the person?	¿Está con la persona?
Did he/she have an accident?	¿Tuvo un accidente?
Is he/she injured?	¿Está lastimado?
Is the person conscious?	¿Está consciente?
Is the person breathing?	¿Está respirando?
Do you know how to give	¿Sabe dar respiración de
mouth-to-mouth resuscitation?	boca a boca?
How does he/she look?	¿Cómo se ve?
Do you hurt?	¿Le duele?
a lot?	mucho?
a little?	poco?
When did the pain start?	¿Cuándo empezó el dolor?
How old is the person?	¿Cuántos años tiene la persona?
Man or woman?	¿Es hombre o mujer?
Is he/she diabetic?	¿Es diabético?
Is he/she taking medicine?	¿Toma medicina?

Is he/she drinking? (alcoholic drinks)	¿Toma bebidas alcohólicas?
The ambulance is coming.	Ya viene la ambulancia.
Calm down.	Cálmese.

II. ACTION SCENE COGNATES

telephone	el teléfono
person	la persona
conscious	consciente
to breathe	respirar
Is he/she breathing?	¿Está respirando?
normally	normalmente
accident	accidente
diabetic	diabético
alcoholic	alcohólico
ambulance	la ambulancia

III. ACTION SCENE VOCABULARY

He/she is	Está
hurt	lastimado
sick	enfermo
conscious	consciente
pain	dolor
Do you hurt?	¿Le duele?
He/she had an accident.	Tuvo un accidente.
Is he/she diabetic?	¿Es diabético?
Is he/she taking medicine?	¿Toma medicina?
Is he/she drinking?	¿Toma bebidas alcóholicas?

Interrogatives

How?	¿Cómo?
How many?	¿Cuántos?
How old is he/she?	¿Cuántos años tiene?

Commands

Calm down.   Cálmese.

IV. EXPANDED VOCABULARY

Does he have . . .	¿Tiene . . .
allergies?	alergías?
difficulty breathing?	dificultad para respirar?
asthma?	asma?
high blood pressure?	presión alta?
ulcers?	úlceras?
heart problems?	problemas del corazón?
high fever?	fiebre alta?
hepatitis?	hepatítus?
kidney problems?	problemas del riñón?
hemophilia?	hemofilia?
broken bones?	fracturas?
epilepsy / seizures?	epilepsia / ataques?
venereal disease?	enfermedad venérea?
AIDS?	el SIDA?
alcohol problems?	problemas con el alcóhol?
drug problems?	problemas con las drogas?
psychological problems?	problemas psicológicos?

V. ACTION SCENE STRUCTURAL EXERCISE

1. 911. (What is your emergency) ¿_____?
2. ¿Está con (the person) _____?
3. ¿Está (injured) _____?
4. ¿Está (conscious) _____?
5. (Is he/she breathing) ¿_____ normalmente?
6. ¿Sabe dar (mouth-to-mouth resuscitation) _____?
7. (Does he hurt) ¿_____?
8. (When) ¿_____ empezó el dolor?
9. ¿Tuvo (an accident) _____?
10. ¿Es (diabetic) _____?

11. ¿Toma (medicine) _____?

12. ¿Toma bebidas (alcoholic) _____?

13. Ya viene (the ambulance) _____.

14. (Calm down) _____.

VI. ACTION SCENE SCENARIOS

1. You are answering a call from a woman who says her husband needs help.

   a. What happened?

   b. What is your name? (optional)

   c. Your address?

   d. Your telephone number?

   e. Are you with the person?

   f. Did he/she have an accident?

2. You are continuing the call described in Scenario 1.

   a. Is he / she injured?

   b. Is the person conscious?

   c. Is the person breathing normally?

   d. Do you know how to give mouth-to-mouth resuscitation?

   e. How does he / she look?

3. You are a dispatcher answering a call from a person who is in need of an ambulance.

   a. Is there pain?

   b. When did the pain start?

   c. How old is the person?

   d. Is it a man or woman?

   e. Is he / she diabetic?

   f. Is he/she taking medicine?

   g. The ambulance is on the way.

CHAPTER 22   EMERGENCY TELECOMMUNICATOR: VIDEO SCRIPT

I. ACTION SCENE: TELECOMMUNICATION OPERATOR

911. What is your emergency?

Your name? (optional)

911. ¿Cuál es su emergencia?

¿Su nombre?

Your address?	¿Su dirección?
Your telephone number?	¿Su teléfono?
Are you with the person?	¿Está con la persona?
Did he/she have an accident?	¿Tuvo un accidente?
Is he/she injured?	¿Está lastimado?
Is the person conscious?	¿Está consciente?
Is the person breathing?	¿Está repirando?
Do you know how to give mouth-to-mouth resuscitation?	¿Sabe dar respiración de boca a boca?
How does he/she look?	¿Cómo se ve?
Do you hurt	¿Le duele
a lot?	mucho?
a little?	poco?
When did the pain start?	¿Cuándo empezó el dolor?
How old is the person?	¿Cuántos años tiene la persona?
Man or woman?	¿Es hombre o mujer?
Is he diabetic?	¿Es diabético?
Is he taking medicine?	¿Toma medicina?
Is he/she drinking? (alcoholic drinks)	¿Toma bebidas alcohólicas?
The ambulance is coming.	Ya viene la ambulancia.
Calm down.	Cálmese.

APPENDIX A

Spanish Pronunciation Guide

THE SOUND SYSTEM

One of the biggest concerns people have about acquiring a second language is speaking with improper pronunciation. Fortunately, Spanish is close enough to English that minor mistakes won't hurt communication. In fact, you need to remember only five sounds in order to speak well enough to be understood. Here are the vowels—each one is pronounced the way it is written:

a (ah) as in yacht, arrest, alert   casa, pasa, masa

e (eh) as in met, methadone, cell   dime, oye, coche

i (ee) as in keep, be, see   licencia, piso, pistola

o (oh) as in open, police   policia, ojo, alto

u (oo) as in spoon, use   uso, utilizar, Humberto

THE VOWELS (SHORT SOUND)

The "a" is similar to the English "a" in "father."

   mamá   casa   alma

The "e" is similar to the English sound in "eight."

   dedo   Delia   déme

The "i" sound is similar to the English "e" in "me."

   sí   Irma   dividir

The "o" sound is similar to the English "o" in the word "no."

   bueno   solo   Pablo

The "u" sound is similar to the English "ue" sound in Susan.

   Lulú   universo   unión

THE CONSONANTS

The "t" is pronounced like the word "stop."

Tomás   tipo   taco

The "d" at the beginning is like the word "David"

día   donde   ándale

The "d" between vowels is similar to the English "th"

todo   Medina   nada

The "j" and "g" before "e" and "i" become similar to the English "h"

gente   Geraldo   jamás

The Spanish "b" and the "v" have no difference in sound. Both are alike. They are similar to the "b" in the word "obedient."

vamos   bote   también

The "y" and the "ll" are the same in most Spanish -speaking countries.

yo   llama   lluvia

The Spanish "r" is pronounced like the English "dd" in the word "fodder."

cara   pero   Laredo

The Spanish "r" at the beginning of the word is trilled ("erre".)

Ricardo   Roberto   Rubén

The Spanish "rr" ("erre") is trilled.

perro   carro   torre

The letter "h" is silent in Spanish.

Hernández   hidalgo   hermano

The Spanish "ñ" is pronounced similar to the word "ca*ny*on."

español   señora   año

¡ No se olvide! (noh seh ohl-'bee-deh) Don't forget!

- Did you notice the accent (´) mark on some words? That part of the word with the accent mark should always be pronounced LOUDER and with more emphasis (i.e., Mamá {mah-'mah}). If there is no accent mark, say the last part of the word LOUDER with more emphasis. (i.e. **doctor** {dohk-'tohr}).

- For words ending in a vowel, or in **n** or **s,** the next to the last part of the word is stressed **excelente** (ehk-seh-'lehn-teh). You'll get the hang of this once you begin to practice.

- In some cases, the letter **u** doesn't make the "oo" sound as with **guitarra** (gee- 'tah-rrah) or **guerra** ('geh-rrah). Don't worry about these words right now. They're few and far between.

---

* **Note:** The word **si** (see) without an accent mark means "if".

> Here's another tip for learners. The trend to mix Spanish and English has created a new language called **"Spanglish".** Millions of immigrants use it so don't be afraid to stick in an English word whenever you forget a Spanish word. Here are a few examples:
>
> **La** "troka"   **La** "ganga"   **El** "hospital"   **El** "bill"

THE SPANISH ALPHABET

At some point during the early stages of learning the language, you may be forced to spell out a word in Spanish. In case of an emergency, you should know the letters of the alphabet in Spanish:

a	(ah)	**n**	('eh-neh)
b	(beh-'grahn-deh)	**ñ**	('eh-nyeh)
c	(seh)	**o**	(oh)
ch	(cheh)	**p**	(peh)
d	(deh)	**q**	(coo)
e	(eh)	**r**	('eh-reh)
f	('eh-feh)	**rr**	('eh-rreh)
g	(heh)	**s**	('eh-seh)
h	('ah-cheh)	**t**	(teh)
i	(ee)	**u**	(oo)
j	('ho-tah)	**v**	(beh-'chee-kah)
k	(kah)	**w**	(doh-bleh-beh)
l	('eh-leh)	**x**	(eh-kees)
ll	('eh-yeh)	**y**	(ee-gree-'eh-gah)
m	('eh-meh)	**z**	('seh-tah)

With each bit of new information, you should be growing in self-confidence. However, if you're still having problems with the sounds of Spanish, try listening to the language for a few minutes each day. Radio, audiocassettes, television, plays, and music performances provide fun and effective ways to help you become familiar with the pronunciation patterns.

COURTESY EXPRESSIONS

Now read these popular expressions and practice them aloud.

Excuse me! (I am leaving)	**¡Con permiso!** (kohn pehr-'mee-soh)
Excuse me!	**¡Perdón!** (pehr-don')
Go ahead!	**¡Pase!** ('pah-seh)

Good afternoon.	**Buenas tardes.** ('bweh-nahs 'tahr-dehs)
Good-bye.	**Adiós.** (ah-dee-'ohs)
Good evening (or good night).	**Buenas noches.** ('bweh-nahs 'noh-chehs)
Good morning.	**Buenos días.** ('bweh-nohs 'dee-ahs)
Hello.	**Hola.** ('oh-lah)
How are you?	**¿Cómo está?** ('koh-oh eh-'stah)
How's it going!	**¡Qué tal!** (keh tahl)
I'm sorry!	**¡Lo siento!** (loh see-'ehn-toh)
May I come in?	**¿Se puede?** (seh 'pweh-deh)
Nice to meet you!	**¡Mucho gusto!** ('moo-choh 'goos-toh)
Please!	**¡Por favor!** (pohr fah-'bohr)
Thank you!	**¡Gracias!** ('grah-see-ahs)
Very well.	**Muy bien.** ('moo-ee 'bee-ehn)
What's happening?	**¿Qué pasa?** (keh 'pah-sah)
What's wrong?/What happened?	**¿Qué pasó?** (keh pah-'soh)
You're welcome!	**¡De nada!** (deh 'nah-dah)

Miranda Warning

Antes de hacerle preguntas, le voy a dar a conocer sus derechos.

Before asking you any questions, I want you to know your rights.

Tiene el derecho de permanecer en silencio.

You have the right to remain silent.

Todo lo que diga puede ser usado en su contra en una corte legal.

Anything you say can be used against you in a court of law.

Tiene el derecho de consultar a un abogado y de tener a su abogado presente durante la interrogación.

You have the right to consult an attorney and to have that attorney present during questioning.

Si no puede pagarle a un abogado, uno le será asignado para que la/lo represente sin cargo, antes y durante la interrogación.

If you are unable to afford an attorney, one will be appointed to represent you without cost, before and during any questioning.

Tiene el derecho de terminar la interrogación en cualquier momento.

You have the right to terminate the questioning at any time.

APPENDIX C

Non-Standard (Slang) Words and Expressions

Give me a break.	Dáme chanza.
cell	el cantón
I am doing (serving) time.	Tirando tiempo.
dude	el vato
dude	el pelado
gang	la carruchas
	gang (Texas)
gang	la ganga
clique	la clica
pals	la Palomilla
the gay person	el joto
the gay person	el puto
the gay person	el maricón
the guard	la melaza
He is doing time.	Está tirando tiempo
He pushed me.	Él me pushó.
I'm working.	Estoy jalando.
identification	la placa
Its over/finished/that's enough	Ya estufas.
jail	el bote
prison	la pinta
kick	kickiar
kicked	kickió

mail, letters	las huilas
Cut me some slack./Give me a break.	Dáme una quebrada.
shower	la playa
tattoo	la copia
brother, best friend	el carnal
wife	la wifa
wife, female boss	la jefa
coffee	el guariche
eatery, to eat	el platón
Let's go eat.	Vamos a refinar.
milk	la leche
paper sack lunch	los juanillos
a hit, shooting	el plomazo
blade	el verduque
shank	el filero
bad ass	el chingón
bully, acts big	el bule
California	Califas
back off, calm down	Aliviánate.
Don't get discouraged.	No te agüites.
See you later.	Ay te washo./Ay te miro.
the main man	el mero mero
big mouth	el hocicón
hairy, long-haired	el peludo
mad looking	el trompudo
Don't cheat me.	No me chingues.

APPENDIX D

Law Enforcement Terminology

A

accident	accidente
accusation	acusación
acuse, to	acusar
arrest	orden de arresto
arrest, to	arrestar
assault	asalta
assailant	asaltante
attorney	abogado

B

bail	fianza
bail bond	contrato de fianza

C

cell	celda
charge	acusar
citizen	ciudadano
city government	municipio
confession	confesión
contraband	contrabando
convict, to	condenar
county	condado
court	corte, tribunal
crime	delito, crimen
criminal	criminal

custody	custodia
custom house	aduana
customs agent	aduanero

D

danger	peligro
dangerous	peligroso
dead	muerto
deportation	deportación
deposition	declaración
detective	detective
document	documento
drug dealer	narcotraficante
drugs	drogas
drunk	borracho

E

emergency	emergencia
evidence	evidencia
expired	vencido

F

fine	multa
firearm	arma de fuego

G

gang	pandilla
green card	tarjeta verde
guard	guardia
guilty	culpable

H

handcuff, to	esposar
handcuffs	esposas
homicide	homicidio

I

identification	identificación
identity	identidad
illegal	ilegal

immigration	inmigración
informant	informante
infraction	infracción
INS	inmigración (la migra)
interrogation	interrogatorio

J

jail	cárcel
judge	juez
judicial	judicial
juvenile	menor de edad

K

kidnapping	secuestro
kill, to	matar
knife	cuchillo, navaja

L

law	ley
lawyer	abogado
legal	legal
license	licencia
license plates	placas

M

minor	menor de edad
misdemeanor	delito menor
murder	asesinato

N

name, first	nombre
name, last	apellido
nickname	apodo
not guilty	inocente, no culpable

O

obey, to	obedecer
officer	oficial
order	orden

P

parole	libertad provisional, libertad vigilada
passenger	pasajero
police	policía
police station	estación de policía
prisoner	prisionero
probation	libertad condicional, libertad vigilada
prosecutor	fiscal
prostitution	prostitución

Q

question	pregunta

R

rape	violación sexual
report	reporte, informe
rights	derechos
robbery	robo

S

safety	seguridad
sample	muestra
search*	registro
search warrant	orden de registro
seat belt	cinturón de seguridad
seize	confiscar
sentence	sentencia
sexual abuse	abuso sexual
sexual assault	asalto sexual
suspect	sospechoso

T

town council	municipio
trial	juicio
trial by jury	juicio por jurado

U

undocumented	indocumentado

*search	revisión (usage may vary)

V

verdict	veredicto
victim	víctima

W

waive	renunciar
warrant	orden
warning	aviso
witness	testigo

Oral Evaluation for Action Scenarios

SCENARIO NAME _____

STUDENT _____

CLASS _____

Excellent	Good	Needs Improvement	
3	**2**	**1**	
			Pronunciation
			Vocabulary
			Mastery of Situation
			Total

Scale

High	8–9
Average	7
Needs practice	6 or below

Instructor Comments:

_____

_____

_____

_____

INDEX

SPANISH ACTION CARDS

The purpose of the Action Cards is to assist the officer while he/she is actually working in a criminal justice environment. The Action Cards are designed to be torn out of this book and placed on the officer's clipboard. The officer can use the card as a prompt, a review, or as a complete series of questions to be asked during an encounter. The cards are designed to solicit mostly yes or no answers, therefore, the officer does not have to be overly concerned with comprehension of a response. If the person does not understand the officer's Spanish statement, and it is a non-hostile encounter, the officer can show the citizen the card and have him/her read the sentence.

Every criminal justice encounter has similar elements present, which are addressed in the Action Cards. There may be times when questions or responses are not presented in the Action Cards. The authors believe this will be the exception rather than the rule.

Action Cards were not produced for encounters where the officer's concentration on safety is so intense that cards would be distracting. The officers are cautioned to use the cards wisely and to not be overly concerned with proper language if safety may be compromised.

MIRANDA WARNING ACTION CARD

Antes de hacerle preguntas, le voy a dar a conocer sus derechos.

Before asking you any questions, I want you to know your rights.

Tiene el derecho de permanecer en silencio.

You have the right to remain silent.

Todo lo que diga puede ser usado en su contra en una corte legal.

Anything you say can be used against you in a court of law.

Tiene el derecho de consultar a un abogado y de tener a su abogado presente durante la interrogación.

You have the right to consult an attorney and to have that attorney present during questioning.

Si no puede pagarle a un abogado, uno le será asignado para que la/lo represente sin cargo, antes y durante la interrogación.

If you are unable to afford an attorney, one will be appointed to represent you without cost, before and during any questioning.

Tiene el derecho de terminar la interrogación en cualquier momento.

You have the right to terminate the questioning at any time.

HOMICIDE ACTION CARD

Soy policía.
I am the police.

¿Quién llamó a la policía?
Who called the police?

¿Cómo se llama?
What is your name?

¿Su dirección?
Your address?

¿Su teléfono durante el día?
Daytime telephone number?

¿Su teléfono durante la noche?
Nighttime telephone number?

¿Su edad?
Age?

¿Su fecha de nacimiento?
Date of birth?

¿Quién es la víctima?
Who is the victim?

¿Dónde está el cuerpo?
Where is the body?

¿Quién descubrió el cuerpo?
Who discovered the body?

¿Cuándo descubrió el cuerpo?
When did you discover the body?

¿Tocó usted el cuerpo?
Did you touch the body?

¿Oyó a alguien peleando?
Did you hear anyone fighting?

¿Oyó disparos?
Did you hear gunshots?

¿Cuántos disparos oyó?
How many shots did you hear?

¿Vio al atacante?
Did you see the attacker?

¿Lo puede identificar?*
Can you identify him?

¿Cuánto mide el atacante?
How tall is the attacker?

¿Cuánto pesa?
How much does he weigh?

¿Adónde fue el atacante?
Where did the attacker go?

¿Vio algún vehículo?
Did you see any vehicle?

¿El color?
The color?

¿El modelo?
The model?

¿El año?
The year?

¿Hay testigos?
Are there witnesses?

Llámenos si tiene más información.
Call us if you have more information.

ROBBERY ACTION CARD

Soy policía.
I am the police.

Es usted la víctima?
Are you the victim?

¿Está lastimada?
Are you hurt?

¿Quién llamó a la policía?
Who called the police?

¿Cómo se llama?
What is your name?

¿Su dirección?
Your address?

¿Su teléfono durante el día?
Daytime telephone number?

¿Su teléfono durante la noche?
Nighttime telephone number?

¿Su edad?
Age?

¿Su fecha de nacimiento?
Date of birth?

¿Qué ocurrió?
What happened?

¿Qué le robaron?
What was robbed?

¿Cuándo ocurrió el robo?
When did the robbery occur?

¿Dónde ocurrió el robo?
Where did the robbery occur?

¿Cuántas personas le robaron?
How many persons robbed you?

¿Conoce al sospechoso?
Do you know the suspect?

¿Lo puede identificar?
Can you identify him?

Describa al sospechoso
Describe the suspect.

¿Qué le dijo el sospechoso?
What did the suspect say to you?

¿Cuánto tiempo estuvo él aquí?
How long was he here?

¿Estaba armado?
Was he armed?

¿Por dónde salió?
Which way did he go?

¿Cuánto cuesta cada cosa?
How much is each item worth?

¿Hay testigos?
Are there witnesses?

Llámenos si tiene más información.
Call us if you have more information.

Soy policía.
I am the police.

¿Quién llamó a la policía?
Who called the police?

¿Está lastimada?
Are you injured?

¿Necesita una ambulancia?
Do you need an ambulance?

Cálmese
Calm down.

Ya viene la ambulancia.
The ambulance is on its way.

¿Cómo se llama?
What is your name?

¿Su dirección?
Your address?

¿Su teléfono durante el día?
Daytime telephone number?

¿Su teléfono durante la noche?
Nighttime telephone number?

¿Su edad?
Age?

¿Su fecha de nacimiento?
Date of birth?

¿Quién le pegó?
Who hit you?

¿Dónde le pegó?
Where were you struck?

¿Cuándo le pegó?
When were you hit?

¿Con qué le pegó?
What did you get hit with?

¿Quiere hacer una denuncia?
Do you wish to file a criminal charge?

¿Le pegó a alguien más?
Did he hit anyone else?

¿Quién pegó primero?
Who struck first?

¿Adónde fue el sospechoso?
Where did the suspect go?

¿Ha tomado usted alcohol?
Have you been drinking?

¿Ha tomado alcohol el sospechoso?
Has the suspect been drinking?

¿Drogas?
Taking drugs?

¿Alguien oyó o vio la pelea?
Did anyone else see or hear the fight?

Voy a hacer un reporte
I am going to make a report.

Llámenos si tiene más información.
Call us if you have more information.

SEXUAL ASSAULT ACTION CARD

Soy policía.

I am the police.

¿Quién llamó a la policía?

Who called the police?

¿Quién es la víctima?

Who is the victim?

¿Está lastimada?

Are you injured?

¿Necesita ayuda?

Do you need help?

¿Necesita ir al hospital?

Do you need to go to a hospital?

¿Cómo se llama?

What is your name?

¿Su dirección?

Your address?

¿Su teléfono durante el día?

Daytime telephone number?

¿Su teléfono durante la noche?

Nighttime telephone number?

¿Su edad?

Age?

¿Su fecha de nacimiento?

Date of birth?

Le voy a hacer unas preguntas difíciles.

I am going to ask you some difficult questions.

¿Cuándo fue el ataque?

When did the attack happen?

¿Dónde fue el ataque?

Where did the attack happen?

¿Conoce al atacante?

Do you know the attacker?

¿Cómo se llama?

What is his name?

¿Su dirección?

His address??

¿A qué cuartos entró?

What rooms did he enter

¿Adónde fue él?

Where did he go?

¿Estaba usted sola?

Were you alone?

¿Pelearon?

Did you fight?

¿El penetró su vagina?

Did he penetrate your vagina?

¿Dónde está la ropa que usted llevaba?

Where are the clothes you were wearing?

Esta ropa puede ser usada como evidencia.

These clothes can be used as evidence.

Describa al atacante.

Describe the attacker

¿Cuánto mide?

How tall is he?

¿Cuánto pesa?

How much does he weigh?

¿Cuántos años tiene?

How old is he?

Llámenos si tiene más información.

Call us if you have more information.

CHILD ABUSE ACTION CARD

Soy policía.

I am the police.

Estamos investigando un reporte de abuso a un niño.

We are investigating a report of child abuse.

¿Cómo se llama?

What is your name?

¿Su dirección?

Your address?

¿Su teléfono durante el día?

Daytime telephone number?

¿Su teléfono durante la noche?

Nighttime telephone number?

¿Su edad?

Age?

¿Su fecha de nacimiento?

Date of birth?

¿Cómo se llama el niño?

What is the name of the child?

¿Cuántos años tiene?

How old is the child?

¿Dónde está el niño?

Where is the child?

Queremos examinar las señas del maltrato en el niño.

We would like to examine the child for signs of child abuse.

¿Cómo se llama usted?

What is your name?

¿Cuál es su relación con el niño?

What is your relation to the child?

¿Cuándo se lastimó el niño?

When was the child injured?

¿Se cayó?

Did he fall down?

¿Tocó algo caliente?

Did he touch something hot?

¿Dónde estaba usted cuando se lastimó el niño?

Where were you when he was injured?

¿Lo llevó al doctor?

Did you take him to the doctor?

¿A la clínica?

to the clinic?

¿Al hospital?

to the hospital?

¿Le pega?

Do you hit the child?

Habrá una investigación.

There will be an investigation.

DOMESTIC DISPUTE ACTION CARD

Soy policía.
I am the police.

¿Está lastimad/a?
Are you hurt?

¿Necesita ayuda?
Do you need help?

¿Necesita un doctor?
Do you need a doctor?

¿Cómo se llama?
What is your name?

¿Su dirección?
Your address?

¿Vive aquí?
Do you live here?

¿Su teléfono durante el día?
Daytime telephone number?

¿Su teléfono durante la noche?
Nighttime telephone number?

¿Su edad?
Age?

¿Su fecha de nacimiento?
Date of birth?

¿Quién le pegó?
Who hit you?

¿Quién más está en la casa?
Who else is in the house?

¿Cuándo le pegó?
Where were you assaulted?

¿Dónde le pegó?
When were you assaulted?

¿Con qué le pegó
What did he hit you with?

¿con la mano?
his hand?

¿con una botella?
a bottle

¿Le pegó a alguien más?
Did he hit anyone else?

¿Dónde está él ahora?
Where is he now?

¿Quiere hacer una denuncia?
Do you want to file charges?

¿Hay testigos?
Are there witnesses?

¿Quiere ir al refugio de mujeres?
Do you want to go to a womens'
    shelter (refuge)?

MISSING PERSON ACTION CARD

Soy policía.
I am the police.

¿Quién llamó a la policía?
Who called the police?

¿Cómo se llama?
What is your name?

¿Su dirección ?
Your address?

¿Su teléfono durante el día?
Daytime telephone number?

¿Su teléfono durante la noche?
Nighttime telephone number?

¿Su edad?
Age?

¿Su fecha de nacimiento?
Date of birth?

¿Quién está perdido?
Who is missing?

¿Cómo se llama?
What is his name?

¿Desde cuándo se perdió?
Since when has he/she been missing?

¿Cuándo (lo, la) vio por última vez?
When did you see her last?

¿Cuántos años tiene?
How old is he/she?

¿Qué ropa llevaba?
What clothing was he/she wearing?

¿Tiene problemas de salud?
Does he/she have any medical problems?

¿Toma medicina?
Is he/she taking medicine?

¿Está con algunos amigos?
Is he/she with any friends?

¿Amenazó con escaparse?
Did he/she threaten to run away?

¿Adónde va con frencuencia (nombre)?
Where does (name) go frequently?

Voy a mandar una descripción a la policía.
I will send a description to the police.

Llámenos si tiene más información.
Contact us if you have more information.

Llámenos si regresa la persona.
Contact us if the person returns.

CURFEW VIOLATION ACTION CARD

Alto.
Stop.

Soy policía.
I am the police.

Ya pasó la hora legal en la calle.
It is past the legal (curfew) hour.

Enséñeme su identificación.
Show me your identification.

¿Cómo se llama?
What is your name?

¿Su dirección?
Your address?

¿Su teléfono durante el día?
Daytime telephone number?

¿Su teléfono durante la noche?
Nighttime telephone number?

¿Su edad?
Age?

¿Su fecha de nacimiento?
Date of birth?

Su conducta es ilegal.
Your conduct is against the law.

¿Dónde están sus padres?
Where are your parents?

Está recibiendo una notificación.
You are being issued a citation.

CRIMINAL TRESPASS ACTION CARD

Soy policia.

I am the police.

¡Escuche!

Listen!

¿Cómo se llama?

What is your name?

¿Su dirección?

Your address?

¿Su teléfono durante el día?

Daytime telephone number?

¿Su teléfono durante la noche?

Nighttime telephone number?

¿Su edad?

Age?

¿Su fecha de nacimiento?

Date of birth?

Aquí tiene un aviso por una entrada ilegal.

Here is a warning for trespassing.

Salga ahora.

Leave now.

No regrese aquí.

Do not come back here.

ARREST FOR CRIMINAL TRESPASS ACTION CARD

Está arrestado por entrar a una zona prohibida.

You are under arrest for criminal trespassing.

Voltéese.

Turn around.

Manos atrás

Hands behind you.

Lo voy a esposar.

I am going to handcuff you.

Vamos a la estación de policía.

We are going to the police station.

BURGLARY ACTION CARD

Soy policía.
I am the police.

¿Quién llamó a la policía?
Who called the police?

¿Cómo se llama?
What is your name?

¿Su dirección?
Your address?

¿Su teléfono durante el día?
Daytime telephone number?

¿Su teléfono durante la noche?
Nighttime telephone number?

¿Su edad?
Age?

¿Su fecha de nacimiento?
Date of birth?

¿A quién le robaron?
Who was burglarized?

¿Quién descubrió el robo?
Who discovered the burglary?

¿Cuándo descubrió el robo?
When was the burglary discovered?

¿Quién es el dueño de la propiedad robada?
Who is the owner of the burglarized property?

¿Qué le robaron?
What was burglarized?

¿Cuánto cuesta cada cosa?
What does each item cost?

¿Tiene el número de serie?
Do you have serial number?

¿El modelo?
The model?

¿Por dónde entraron?
Where did they enter?

¿Cómo entraron?
How did they break in?

¿Estaba sola la casa?
Was the house unoccupied?

¿Desde cuándo?
Since when?

¿Vio a alguien?
Did you see anyone?

¿Sospecha de alguien?
Do you suspect anyone?

¿Ha tocado usted algo?
Have you touched anything?

Voy a tomar las huellas digitales.
I am going to take fingerprints.

¿Hay testigos?
Are there witnesses?

Llámenos si tiene más información.
Call us if you have information.

THEFT ACTION CARD

Soy policía.
I am the police.

¿Quién llamó a la policía?
Who called the police?

¿Cómo se llama?
What is your name?

¿Su direcion?
Your address?

¿Su teléfono durante el día?
Daytime telephone number?

¿Su teléfono durante la noche?
Nighttime telephone number?

¿Su edad?
Age?

¿Su fecha de nacimiento?
Date of birth?

¿Le robaron algo?
Did you have something stolen?

¿Qué le robaron?
What was stolen?

¿Algo más?
Anything else?

¿Cuándo le robaron?
When were they stolen?

¿Dónde le robaron?
Where were they stolen?

¿Cómo le robaron?
How were the item(s) stolen?

¿Dónde estaba cuando le robaron?
Where were you when the property was stolen?

¿Sospecha de alguien?
Do you suspect anyone?

¿Vio a alguien cerca?
Did you see anyone nearby?

¿Hay testigos?
Are there witnesses?

Llámenos si tiene más información.
Call us if you have more information.

MOTOR VEHICLE THEFT ACTION CARD

Soy policía.
I am the police

¿Quién llamó a la policía?
Who called the police?

¿Cómo se llama?
What is your name?

¿Su dirección?
Your address?

¿Su teléfono durante el día?
Daytime telephone number?

¿Su teléfono durante la noche?
Nighttime telephone number?

¿Su fecha de nacimiento?
Date of birth?

Dónde trabaja?
Where do you work?

¿De quién es el vehículo robado?
Who is the owner of the stolen vehicle?

Describa el vehículo.
Describe the vehicle.

¿el color?
the color

¿la marca?
the brand? (make)

¿el modelo?
the model?

¿Algún daño visible?
Any visible damage?

¿El número de la placa?
The license plate number?

¿Quién vio por última vez el vehículo?
Who saw it last?

¿Cuándo fue eso?
When was that?

¿Quién descubrió que no estaba?
Who discovered that it was missing?

¿Cuándo descubrió que no estaba?
When was it discovered missing?

¿Dónde estaba estacionado?
Where was it parked?

¿Alguien más tiene las llaves?
Does anyone else have the keys?

¿Está pagado el vehículo?
Is the vehicle paid for?

¿Tiene seguro?
Do you have insurance?

¿Con quién?
With whom?

Voy a hacer un reporte.
I am going to make a report.

Llámenos si tiene más información.
Call us if you have more information.

CRIMINAL MISCHIEF VANDALISM ACTION CARD

Soy policía.
I am the police.

¿Quién llamó a la policía?
Who called the police?

¿Cómo se llama?
What is your name?

¿Su dirección?
Your address?

¿Su teléfono durante el día?
Daytime telephone number?

¿Su teléfono durante la noche?
Nighttime telephone number?

¿Su fecha de nacimiento?
Date of birth?

¿Dónde trabaja?
Where do you work?

¿Cuándo descubrió el daño?
When was the damage discovered?

¿Quién descubrió el daño?
Who discovered the damage?

¿Cuánto costará reparar la propiedad?
How much will it cost to repair the property?

¿Sospecha de alguien?
Do you suspect anyone?

¿De quién?
If so, who?

¿Dónde vive?
Where does he/she live?

¿Hay testigos?
Are there witnesses?

Voy a escribir un reporte.
I will write a report.

Llámenos si tiene más preguntas o más información.
Call us if you have more questions or more information.

DRIVING WHILE INTOXICATED DUI ACTION CARD

Soy la policía.

I am the police.

Salga del vehículo.

Step out of the vehicle.

Fue detenida por no manejar en línea recta.

You were stopped for not driving in a straight line.

Enséñeme. . .

Show me your. . .

su licencia de manejar

driver's license

sus papeles del registro

car registration

sus papeles del seguro

insurance papers

¿Toma medicina?

Are you taking medicine?

¿Para que?

What for?

¿A qué hora tomó la medicina?

At what time did you take medicine last?

¿Ha tomado alcohol?

Have you been drinking alcohol?

¿Cuántas bebidas alcohólicas tomó?

How many drinks did you have?

¿A qué hora empezó a tomar?

At what time did you start drinking?

¿A qué hora tomó la última bebida alcohólica?

When was your last drink?

¿Ha fumado marijuana?

Have you smoked marijuana?

¿Toma otra droga?

Are you on any other drugs?

¿Dónde está ahora?

Where are you right now?

¿Qué hora es?

What time is it now?

Voy a hacerle una prueba de alcohol.

I am going to give you an alcohol test.

Está arrestado.

You are under arrest.

Su coche será detenido.

Your car will be detained.

HORIZONTAL GAZE NYSTAGMUS (HGN)

Quítese los lentes.

Remove your sunglasses.

¿Usa lentes de contacto?

Are you wearing contact lenses?

Mire la punta de mi pluma/mi lápiz.

Look at the tip of my pen/my pencil.

¿Puede ver mi pluma?/mi lápiz?

Can you see my pen?/my pencil?

Siga el instrumento con sus ojos.

Follow the instrument with your eyes.

No mueva la cabeza.

Do not move your head.

Haga la prueba.

Do the test.

Voy a repetir la prueba.

I will repeat the test.

FINGER TO NOSE TEST ACTION CARD

Párese derecho.

Stand straight.

Ponga sus pies juntos.

Put your feet together.

Voy a demostrarle la prueba.

I will demonstrate for you.

Extienda sus brazos.

Extend your arms.

Mire hacia arriba.

Look up.

Toque la nariz con el dedo de la mano derecha.

Touch your nose with a finger of your right hand.

Toque la nariz con el dedo de la mano izquierda.

Touch your nose with a finger of your left hand.

¿Tiene preguntas?

Do you have any questions?

Cierre los ojos.

Close your eyes.

Haga la prueba.

Do the test.

ONE LEG STAND TEST ACTION CARD

Párese derecho.

Stand erect.

Ponga sus brazos a los lados.

Put your arms to the side.

Se lo voy a demostrar.

I will demonstrate for you.

Levante su pierna (derecha, izquierda) como seis pulgadas.

Raise your (right, left) leg about 6″.

Cuente de uno hasta treinta.

Count from 1 to 30

Haga la prueba.

Do the test.

¿Tiene preguntas?

Do you have questions?

WALKING HEEL TO TOE TEST ACTION CARD

¿Tiene algún problema en su espalda?

Do you have a problem with your back?

¿Tiene algún problema en sus piernas?

Do you have a problem with your leg?

¿Tiene algún problema en sus pies?

Do you have a problem with your feet?

Dé (cuatro/cinco/seis/siete) pasos con un pie detrás del otro.

Take 4,5,6,7 steps one foot in front of the other.

Cuando dé el último paso, voltéese en su pie (izquierdo/ derecho).

When you have taken the last step, pivot on your (right, left) foot back heel to toe.

Regrese (cuatro/cinco/seis/siete) pasos con un pie detrás del otro.

Walk 4,5,6,7 steps back heel to toe.

Camine en línea recta.

Walk in a straight line.

Mantenga sus manos y sus brazos a los lados.

Keep your hands and arms to your side.

Manténgase erguido / derecho.

Do not hold on to yourself .

No se recargue en nada.

Do not hold on to other objects to balance.

Cuente cada paso.

Count as you take each step.

Voy a demostrarle.

I will demonstrate for you.

Haga la prueba.

Do the test.

¿Tiene preguntas?

Do you have any questions?

LOW RISK TRAFFIC STOP ACTION CARD

Soy policía.

I am the police.

¿Tiene una emergencia?

Do you have an emergency?

Déme su licencia de manejar.

Give me your driver's license.

Déme sus papeles del seguro.

Give me your insurance papers.

Déme sus papeles del registro.

Give me your registration papers.

Salga del vehículo.

Step out of the vehicle.

Cierre la puerta.

Close the door.

Saque sus manos de los bolsillos.

Take your hands out of your pockets.

¿De quién es el vehículo?

Who is the owner of this vehicle?

¿Qué año?

The year?

¿Qué marca?

The make?

Va a recibir una notificación de una infracción.

You are going to receive citation of an infraction.

Firme aquí.

Sign here.

No está admitiendo su culpabilidad.

You are not admitting your guilt.

Su firma es una promesa de que va a comunicarse con el juez durante el tiempo indicado.

This is a promise to contact the judge within the time indicated.

Tenga precaución.

Take precaution.

Tenga cuidado.

Be careful.

¿Es usted el conductor del vehículo?
Are you the driver of the car?

¿Está lastimado?
Is anyone injured?

Enséñeme . . .
Show me . . .

su licencia de manejar
your driver's license

sus papeles del seguro
your insurance papers

sus papeles del registro
car registration papers

¿Es correcta la información en su licencia?
Is the information correct on your license?

¿Su teléfono?
Your telephone number?

¿Dónde trabaja?
Where do you work?

¿Quién estaba manejando el vehículo?
Who was driving the vehicle?

¿A qué hora ocurrió el accidente?
At what time did the accident occur?

¿Llovía?
Was it raining?

¿En qué calle estaba?
What street were you on?

¿Estaba tratando de doblar?
Were you trying to turn?

¿Hizo alguna señal?
Did you signal the turn?

¿De dónde venía el otro vehículo?
Where did the other vehicle come from?

¿A qué velocidad iba?
How fast were you going?

¿El semáforo estaba rojo?
Was the traffic light red?

amarillo?
yellow?

o verde?
green?

¿Se detuvo?
Did you stop?

¿Se detuvo el otro vehículo?
Did the other vehicle stop?

¿Había un problema mecánico en su vehículo?
Was there a mechanical problem?

¿Se puso el cinturón de seguridad?
Were you wearing your seat belt?

¿Es posible manejar su vehículo?
Is it possible to drive the vehicle?

Ya viene la grúa.
A tow truck is coming.

Va a recibir una notificación por una infracción.
You are receiving a citation for an infraction.

CONSENT SEARCH ACTION CARD

Soy policía.
I am the police.

Saque las manos de sus bolsillos.
Take your hands out of your pockets.

¿Adónde va?
Where are you going?

¿De dónde viene usted?
Where are you coming from?

¿Desde cuándo está viajando?
How long have you been travelling?

¿De quién es el vehículo?
Whose vehicle is this?

¿Cada cuándo le pone gasolina?
How often do you put gasoline in it
(the vehicle)?

Abra la cajuela.
Open the trunk.

¿Tiene aire su llanta de refacción?
Does your spare tire have air?

¿Tiene drogas en el vehículo?
Do you have drugs in the vehicle?

¿Tiene armas en el vehículo?
Do you have weapons in the vehicle?

Párese allá.
Stand there.

Soy policía.
I am the police.

Está arrestado.
You are under arrest.

No voltee.
Do not turn around.

No se mueva.
Do not move.

Ponga las manos sobre su cabeza.
Place your hands on your head.

Con la mano izquierda apague el motor.
With your left hand turn off the ignition.

¡Hágalo ahora!
DO IT NOW!

Con la mano izquierda abra la ventana.
With your left hand roll down your window.

Con la mano izquierda tire las llaves hacia mi voz.
With your left hand, throw the keys towards the sound of my voice.

¡Abra la puerta!
Open the door.

Salga del vehículo.
Step out of the vehicle.

Mantenga sus manos arriba.
Keep your hands up high.

Aléjese dos pasos del vehículo hacia su izquierda/derecha.
Take two steps away from the vehicle toward your left/right.

Con la mano izquierda levante la parte de atrás de su camisa.
With your left hand lift the back of your shirt.

Voltéese despacio.
Turn around slowly.

Alto.
Stop.

Siga.
Keep on (turning).

Camine para atrás hacia mi voz.
Walk backward toward my voice.

De rodillas.
Kneel down.

Ponga sus manos sobre la cabeza.
Place your hands on your head.

Cruce sus dedos de las manos.
Interlock your fingers.

¿Tiene armas?
Do you have any weapons?

Levántese.
Get up.

SUSPICIOUS PERSON ACTION CARD

Venga aquí.
Come here.

¿Qué pasa?
What is going on?

Saque las manos de sus bolsillos.
Take your hands out of your pockets.

Quédese aquí.
Stay here.

No se mueva.
Do not move.

Déme su identificación.
Show me your identification.

¿Cómo se llama?
What is your name?

¿Su dirección?
Your address?

¿Su teléfono durante el día?
Daytime telephone number?

¿Su edad?
Your age?

¿Su fecha de nacimiento?
Date of birth?

¿Dónde trabaja?
Where do you work?

¿Adónde va?
Where are you going?

¿Vive aquí?
Do you live here?

¿Está esperando a un amigo?
Are you waiting for a friend?

¿Desde cuándo?
Since when?

¿Cómo se llama su amigo?
What is your friend's name?

¿Tiene usted armas?
Do you have any weapons.

Lo voy a revisar.
I am going to search you.

Voltéese.
Turn around.

Está arrestado.
You are under arrest.

Manos sobre la cabeza.
Hands over your head.

Separe las piernas.
Separate your legs.

Lo voy a esposar.
I am going to handcuff you.

Saque todo de sus bolsillos.
Take everything out of your pockets

Ponga todo aquí.
Place the things here.

Siéntese.
Sit down.

¿Por qué está arrestada?
Why have you been arrested?

¿Cómo se llama?
What is your name?

¿su dirección?
your address?

¿su teléfono durante el día?
daytime telephone number?

¿su fecha de nacimiento?
date of birth?

¿Dónde nació?
Where were you born?

¿Dónde trabaja?
Where do you work?

Párese aquí, por favor.
Stand here, please.

¿Es usted ciudadana/o de este país?
Are you a citizen of this country?

¿Cuál es el número de su seguro social?
What is your social security number?

¿Cuánto mide usted?
How tall are you?

¿Cuánto pesa usted?
How much do you weigh?

¿En caso de emergencia, a quién podemos llamar?
Who do we contact in case of an emergency?

¿Cuál es la dirección de esa persona?
What is that person's address?

¿Cuál es el número de teléfono de esa persona?
What is that person's telephone number?

¿Lo/la han arrestado antes?
Have you ever been arrested before?

¿Dónde?
Where?

¿Por qué?
Why?

¿Cuando?
When?

¿Ha estado en esta cárcel antes?
Have you been in this jail before?

Esta es una lista de las propiedades que tenemos bajo custodia.
This is a list of the property we have in custody.

Si es correcta, firme aquí.
If it is correct, sign here.

¿Quiere llamar a alguien?
Do you want to call someone?

Aquí está el teléfono.
Here is the telephone.